ADVANTAGES OF RE-MARRIAGE IN DALIT CASTES

ADVANTAGES OF RE-MARRIAGE IN DALIT CASTES

By
Dr. Akansha Chaudhary
&
Dr. Neelma Kunwar
Officer Incharge
Deptt. of Extension Communication Management
Faculty of Home Science
C.S. Azad University of Agriculture & Technology
Kanpur (UP)

DISCOVERY PUBLISHING HOUSE PVT. LTD.
NEW DELHI-110 002

Published by:
Tilak Wasan

DISCOVERY PUBLISHING HOUSE PVT. LTD.
4831/24, Prahlad Street, Ansari Road
Darya Ganj, New Delhi-110002 (India)
Phone: +91-11-23279245, 43764432
Fax: +91-11-23253475
E-mail: parul.wasan@gmail.com
           info@discoverypublishinggroup.com
           web: www.discoverypublishinggroup.com

First Edition: **2011**
ISBN: 978-81-8356-871-5

Advantages of Re-marriage in Dalit Castes
© 2011, **Authors**

All rights reserved. No part of this publication should be reproduced, stored in a retrieval system, or transmitted in any form or by any means: electronic, mechanical, photocopying, recording or otherwise, without the prior written permission of the author and the publisher.

This book has been published in good faith that the material provided by authors is original. Every effort is made to ensure accuracy of material, but the publisher and printer will not be held responsible for any inadvertent error(s). In case of any dispute, all legal matters are to be settled under Delhi jurisdiction only.

Preface

Dalit consider themselves as part of Hindu society, many of their social character do not resemble Hindu Social character may be perhaps they retained certain portion of the original Austric or Dravidian social systems. One of the striking difference is the position of women in their society; though it has changed in respect of many.

There are about 250 million dalits in India. There is meager improvement in the socio-economic condition of dalits in the past 50 years, which is not enough when compared to non-dalits, of course, much more needs to be done. The urgent need is to have a national sample survey on dalits. Every fourth Indian is a dalit. There is no proper survey to give the correct number of dalit women in India. They are generally scattered in villages and they are not a monogamous group. About 75 per cent dalits live below poverty line. Economic backwardness of dalits is mostly due to injustice done to them by the high castes and also due to exploitation. From the time immemorial they worked like slaves, sold as commodities resulting in their social discrimination, economic deprivation and educational backwardness.

One of the important reason for dalit women having better position than those of higher caste being, dalit women had to go for wage earning due to high rate of poverty. As wage earners obviously they had better respect since family had to depends at least partly on their income. It is not so in general in respect of women of higher caste where in they are considered as took of six. In respect of dalit crafts man like the chamars, women participate in production.

Dalit women has most horrible position in Indian society even today, though the rigidity of untouchability had been relaxed to many extend, but status remained almost some. Women are compelled to go for hard labour with discrimination of wages, sexually abused frequently and have to go for most dirty and odd jobs. They are not permitted to wear decent dresses and ornaments even if they can afford. While society extract all the necessary services, it look down as downtrodden. It becomes greatest joke when Indian criticise whites from Sough Africa for the apartheid while they themselves practice untouchability which is many time more than apartheid. As dalit women know their difficult and hard life, so they easily accept re-marriage. Re-marriage is socially accepted in dalit castes. Great leader like Dr. B.R. Ambedkar, Mahatma Gandhi, Raja Ram Mohan Roy also supported re-marriage. So dalit women do not hesitate to accept it. Re-marriage is not a social evil for dalit women. They consider fruitful it for their deserted and isolated life in the form of economical, social security and psychological support. So re-marriage is socially accepted in dalit castes and dalit women do not feel themselves ashamed due to re-marriage. So they have positive opinion about re-marriage due to social acceptance in their society and they positively accept it also.

Authors

Acknowledgements

My debts are great and too many, which I cannot even dare to acknowledge, especially of almighty God, who bestowed on me the courage to carry out this research work.

It is a golden opportunity and proud privilege to work under the most talented and inspiring guidance of Dr. Neelma Kunwar (D.Sc.), Officer In-charge, Department of Extension Education and Communication Management, C.S. Azad University of Agriculture and Technology, Kanpur and Chairperson of my advisory committee. Her untiring supervision, persistent encouragement, unending zeal, conspicuous ability and constructive criticism have always been a constant source of my inspiration and achievements. I am extremely indebted to her for being meticulous throughout investigation and preparation of this manuscript.

I also express my heartfelt thanks and gratitude to Dr. Rekha Dayal, Officer In-charge, Department of family Resource Management, College of Home Science, Dr. R.N. Prasad (Retd.) Associate Professor (Statistics, Department of Agricultural Economics and Statistics and Dr. Mukesh Srivastava, Associate Professor, Department of Plant Pathology C.S. Azad University of Agriculture and Technology, Kanpur who are the members of my advisory committee, for their effluent efforts, timely guidance and creative suggestions during the tenure of the presents study.

Words can never express the indebtedness but, I dare to take this opportunity to pay my sincere appreciation to Mr. Arun Kumar Srivastava, Assistant Statistician, Department of Crop Physiology, C.S. Azad University of agriculture and

Technology, Kanpur for not only helping me but also took keen interest throughout the course of investigation. Had they not taken painstaking efforts and inspiring attitudes, this research work would not have been accomplished.

I am equally obliged and express my veneration to Ms. Renuka Singh, Teacher, Department of ECM, C.S. Azad University of Agriculture and Technology, Kanpur who co-operated me during my study period.

I am also thankful to Dr. Ram Charan, Director of Extension, C.S. Azad University of Agriculture and Technology, Kanpur and Dr. P.K. Rathi, Associate Director, Directorate of Extension, C.S. Azad University of Agriculture and Technology, Kanpur for their kind co-operation and best wishes during my study period. It is very difficult task for me to search appropriate words and express my sincere appreciation to Dr. Santosh Kumar Vishwakarm, Programme Co-ordinate, K.V.K. Lakhimpur Kheri, for providing precious guidance and full co-operation during my study period.

From the core of my heart, uncountable words of cordial veneration and gratitude are dedicated to the pious feet of my paternal grand father (Late) Sri Bankey Lal, my grand mother (Late) Smt. Kamla, my maternal grand father Sri. Sukhwasi lal and grand mother Mrs. Suryankanti, my father Shri. P.C. Chaudhary and my mother Mrs. Manju Lata Chaudhary for their love, affection good wishes, blessings, constant encouragement and inspiration, showered upon me for the achievements of my present educational assets. I also express my warmest appreciation to my brother Avinash and Mrityunjaya and Younger Sister Sanvedna for their never ending love and best whishes.

I am also thankful to my Mausaji Sri Ram Milan Choudhary and Mausi Ji Mrs. Sushma Chaudhary, who extended moral support, timely help and constant inspiration to me during my research work.

My heartful emotions from my core of heart are due to my beloved uncle Sri. Balveer and Aunty Mrs. Rani for their moral support throught my study period.

I very humbly express my most sincere of profound sense of gratitude and veneration to my Mama Ji and Mami Ji, Dr. Vinod and Mrs. Meera, Sri. Devendra and Mrs. Bhagyawati, Mr. Manoj and Shilpa and Mr. Jitendra and Mrs. Seema without whose inspiration I could not achieve such type of opportunity.

I am getting short of words to express my special thanks to my all loving cousins specially Brijesh who co-operated me in my bad times and helped me to overcome my mental tiredness and distress.

I am also grateful for the enormous affection, constant encouragement, cordial support and best wishes extended by those whose presence one can feel always at the hour of need. Their love and moral support helped me cope up with problems and showed me the path to success.

I offer my warmest thanks and indebtedness to my friends; Sweta, Varsha, Yogesh and all others, for thier constant love, help and encouragement.

Akansha Chaudhary

Contents

Preface

Acknowledgements

1. **Introduction** 1

   Role of Dalit Women in Indian Society—Socio-economic Conditions of Dalit Women—Economic Development of Dalit Women According to Occupation—Views of Women about Re-marriage—What is Re-marriage—Impact of Re-marriage in Indian Society—Social Impact—Impact of Re-marriage with Family and Child Support—Economic Impact—Psychological Impact—Advantages of Re-marriage—Promoting Factors of Re-marriage in Dalit Castes—Objectives—Justification of the Study.

2. **Review of Literature** 15

3. **Profile of the Study Area** 31

   District Kanpur—Location—Area—Population—Climate—Rainfall—Temperature—Humidity—Selected Sample of Kanpur City.

4. **Research Methodology** 35

   Research Design—Variables and their Measurements—Period of Investigation—Statistical Techniques.

5. **Findings and Discussion** 44

   I. Socio-economic Status of Dalit Caste Women—Education—Type of Family—Family Size—Type of House—Family Income—Sub Caste—Religion—Occupation—Marital Status—Economic Status—

Material Possession—II. Views of the Respondents Regarding Re-marriage—Promoting Factors for Re-marriage of Dalit Castes—A. Social Factors—B. Cultural Factors—C. Religious Factors—D. Other Factors—III. Impact of Sociological, Economic and Psychological Status of Dalit Women Regarding Re-marriage.

6. **Summary and Conclusion** 88

   Objectives—Research Methodology—Major Findings—Suggestions, Recommendation and Policy Implications.

   Bibliography 97

   Index 103

CHAPTER 1

Introduction

The LORD God said, *"It is not good for the man to be alone, I will make a helper suitable for him/her."*

There are about 250 million *dalits* in India. There is meager improvement in the socio-economic condition of *dalits* in the past over 60 years, which is not enough when compared to non-*dalits*. Of course, much more needs to be done. The urgent need is to have a national sample survey on *dalits*. Every fourth Indian is a *dalit*. There is no proper survey to give the correct number of *dalit* women in India. They are generally scattered in villages and they are not a monogamous group. About 75 per cent *dalits* live below poverty line. Economic backwardness of *dalits* is mostly due to injustice done to them by the high castes and also due to exploitation. From the time immemorial they worked like slaves, sold as commodities resulting in their social discrimination, economic deprivation and educational backwardness.

Dalit consider themselves as part of Hindu society, many of their social character do not resemble Hindu social character may be perhaps they retained certain portion of the original Austric or Dravidian social systems. One of the striking difference is the position of women in their society; though it has changed in respect of many.

Much before Pandit Ishwar Chandra Vidyasagar propagated widow re-marriage among Hindus, these people had recognition of widow re-marriage though such marriages has no rituals. Even divorce and marriage of divorce was not rare. Even during hay day of widow burning in Bengal prior or Raja Rammohan Roy, *sati* was rarely practised by these castes though it was not totally absent, *sati* was found in rare occasions in those areas where population of lower caste Hindu was predominantly more. (Here higher caste Hindu refers to Brahmin, Khatriya Vaishya and Sat-Sudras like Kayastha and Vaishya).

Dr. B.R. Ambedkar, Raja Rammohan Roy, Pandit Ishwar Chandra Vidyasagar, Mahatma Phule etc., the great social reformers supported re-marriage either it is widow or deserted women. Raja Rammohan Roy married a widow women thus setting the example for the whole society. He openly favoured the concept of re-marriage of women. Widow is the worst condition of women in the society in comparison of deserted women. So these great social reformers gave support to re-marriage.

In spite of adopting patriarchiacal society, women had say in every matter in the house and society in a total contrast to higher caste Hindus. They were often consulted and participate in decision making.

One of the important reason for *dalit* women having better position than those of higher caste being, *dalit* women had to go for wage earning due to high rate of poverty. As wage earner obviously they had better respect since family had to depend at least partly on their income. It is not so in general in respect of women of higher caste wherein they are considered as tool of sex. In respect of *dalit* craftsman like the *chamars*, women participate in production.

The present positions seems to be better with reference to the rate of literacy among *dalit*s. The literacy rate is 31.48 per cent for boys and 10.93 per cent for girls. The *dalits* women belonging to the creamy layer of the society are better with good education and socially and economically they are well off like other high castes. They are fully aware of the welfare schemes provided by the Government and their percentage is very low when compared with the total *dalit* population. In rural areas, the first generation girls from scheduled caste needs the attention of Government and other organization. Mostly the teachers of the locality provide information to them about the welfare schemes. In many *dalit* association executive position are occupied by male members whereas very poor representation is made by women in their past. The women are not properly informed about the Government schemes and there is an urgent need to get a feedback about the welfare schemes where lot of money is spent for the development of *dalits*. The funds are not utilized properly for their upliftment. Many of the schemes go unnoticed because they are not popularized properly.

Role of *Dalit* Women in Indian Society

Dalit women are compelled to go for various economic activities primarily due to these economic condition. Even they go for hard labour, which are supposed to be done by men. But they used to get less wages in comparison to their male counter-part. While Bagdi men earn as security men or as musician (they used to play drums during festive occasions) women work as daily labour for threshing paddy, transplanting seedlings or even as labour in road or building construction. Construction workers often become victim lust of contractors, mostly of higher caste Hindu, Muslims or Christians, many time raped. Before advancement of medical science, maternity job used to be the work of Hadi women. Though normally considered as untouchables, these women were permitted to enter the inside of the houses at the time of child birth. After jobs are over they are reverted back to the untouchable status.

Dalit women have most horrible position in Indian society even today, though the rigidity of untouchability had been relaxed to many extent, but status remained almost same. Women are compelled to go for hard labour with discrimination of wages, sexually abused frequently and have to go for most dirty and odd jobs. They are not permitted to wear decent dresses and ornaments even if they can afford. While society extract all the necessary services, it look down as downtrodden. It becomes greatest joke when Indian criticise whites from South Africa for the apartheid while they themselves practice untouchability which is many time more than apartheid.

It is generally considered that the *dalits* are the lowest strata of Hindu society. In other words they are considered as part of Hindu society. It is believed so in spite of the fact that they are not considered as equals with other Hindu cousins. Even Brahmin priests do not serve them in respect of their various rituals. That means they are not permitted to follow Hindu rituals though they are considered as part of Hindu society. This only shows they are considered as Hindu not for their advantage but to the extent of the advantage of caste Hindu only.

The highest number of scheduled castes is found in Uttar Pradesh (22.3% of the total scheduled castes population in the country), followed by West Bengal (11.4%), Bihar (9.6%), Tamil Nadu (8.5%), Andhra Pradesh (7.6%), Madhya Pradesh (7.0%), Rajasthan (5.6%), Karnataka (5.3%), Punjab (4.3%) and Maharashtra (4.3%). Thus, about two-thirds of the scheduled castes (66.4%) live in six States only.

Socio-economic Conditions of *Dalit* Women

About 84 per cent of the scheduled castes people live in rural areas as agricultural labour, share croppers, tenants and marginal farmers. Almost all persons engaged in jobs like sweeping scavenging and tanning belong to the scheduled castes.

In rural scenario *dalits* being untouchable are allowed to settled either in terms of work/occupations, according to the 2001 Census, of the total scheduled castes population of 1,047 lakh persons, 441.8 lakhs (42.2%) fall in the category of workers. Of these, 53.8 per cent are working as leather-workers, 12.4 per cent weavers, 7.9 per cent as fisherman, 6.8 per cent as toddy-toppers, 5.2 per cent as basket/rope makers, 4.6 per cent as washermen, 3.7 per cent as scavengers, 1.3 per cent as artisans, 1.3 per cent as fruit/vegetable sellers, 0.9 per cent as drummers, 0.1 per cent as carpenters and iron-smiths, and 1.3 per cent are engaged in some other petty occupation.

About two-thirds of the bonded labourers are from scheduled castes. Literacy among the scheduled castes people is extremely low. It was only 21.4 per cent in 1981 as against the all India average of 41.3 per cent (excluding scheduled castes and scheduled tribes). Most of them live below the poverty line and are the victims of social and economic exploitation. In theory, untouchability might have been abolished but in practice, these people continue to be subject of discrimination.

In rural scenario being untouchable are allowed to settled either in a colony outside the village of upper castes or have separate villages of their own. Among various *dalit* castes again there is untouchability among themselves. For examples – bhangis used to be considered as untouchable by others, chamars are considered untouchable by many other and so on. Therefore, within untouchable colonies in a village there used to be separate colonies for each *dalit* community due to such social taboos. After untouchability could be diminished and finally removed after independence due constitutional provision, the status quo of the colony or type of colonies continued. Therefore in rural back drop the *dalit* communities are normally found settled in clusters.

The economic condition of the sudras also reveals the low position that they occupied in the hierarchy of society. The cases of Sudras possessing cattle and health were very rare. Mostly they worked as landless labourers on farms and as domestic servants. One *sutra* mentions that "Sudras have to earn their subsistence only by serving the higher *varnas*."

Economic Development of *Dalit* Women According to Occupation

The occupation of many scheduled castes women can be divided in the following heads :

1. Agricultural labour
2. Marginal cultivators
3. Fisherwomen
4. Traditional artisans
5. Leather workers
6. Weavers
7. Scavengers and sweepers
8. Midwifery
9. Beedi factories and unorganized sectors.

The Work Participation Rate (WPR) of scheduled castes population is said to be 22.25 per cent for males and 25.98 per cent for females.

The contribution of scheduled castes women to the economic development of our country is significant especially in the agricultural sector. They are exploited by the higher caste landlords. They are paid very marginal salary for the hard work in the field for the whole day. In leather industries the tanning process is considered to be an unclean job which is done only by socially backward class. Traditional artistes get very more benefit because the middleman exploits them. The condition of scavenger and sweepers is very deplorable and they are most vulnerable sectors among scheduled castes. The working condition is very poor and the remuneration is also very poor.

The scheduled castes are largely concentrated in rural areas and 95 per cent of them (including 35 per cent agricultural labourers) derive their sustenance from agriculture. In most villages, they continue to suffer residential segregation. Those who have changed their traditional occupation face less status disabilities. In some cases, however, they suffer because of their hereditary identity. Their ascriptive status scores over their achieved status. The betterment of their conditions, thus, seems to be nowhere nearer solution. Politically, through they have become conscious of the value of their vote for election, yet they have not succeeded in transforming the larger system, so that its processes could usher in effective social economic and political equality.

Views of Women about Re-marriage

As *dalit* women know their difficult and hard life, so they easily accept re-marriage. Re-marriage is socially accepted in *dalit* castes. Great leaders like Dr. B.R. Ambedkar, Mahatma Gandhi, Raja Ram Mohan Roy also supported re-marriage. So *dalit* women do not hesitate to accept it. Re-marriage is not a social evil for *dalit* women. They consider fruitful it for their deserted and isolated life in the form of economical, social security and psychological support. So re-marriage is socially accepted in *dalit* castes and *dalit* women do not feel themselves ashamed due to re-marriage. So they have positive opinion about re-marriage due to social acceptance in their society and they positively accept it also.

What is Re-marriage

Re-marriage is just another chance that you give yourself to live a fulfilling life that gives you back your self-esteem, confidence and desire to be who you are!

Re-marriage provides social support, encourages companionship and communication. By the time people remarry, they have gained some maturity from their experience in their first marriage and thus are more likely to be more open and expressive about certain issues. Re-marriage can actually soothe ruffled feathers and unite love between two hearts that have unfortunately seen more of the seamier side of marriage. In fact, re-marriage may actually be the beginning of a more meaningful life, and make two people live a true marriage which will never crumble. It can make re-married couples happy and satisfied people in later-life.

Men and women today are ready to make a change in their situation, if they do not find it agreeable. Those who have got over their past marriage or the loss of a spouse and are ready to move forward and ring the bells of re-marriage, can share their concerns with their prospective partners if any, about each other's relationship with their ex, relationship with ex in-laws, child support payments and so on and understand the complexities with the challenges of blending two families-with or without children. They can work at forging positive relationships among family members on their re-marriage.

It is important to think it out, plan it and shrug off the bad influences and habits that had affected the previous relationship. It is equally important to steer clear of the shadows of the past, avoid mistakes in the past relationship and refrain from berating.

Impact of Re-marriage in Indian Society

As re-marriage is accepted in *dalit* castes due to social economical factors. It is really beneficial for *dalit* women. As *dalit* women has most horrible position in Indian society even today, suffers from molestation etc. It is better to remarry and have a protected life. This protection may be social economical and psychological also, because due to re-marriage *dalit* women get economical support by their husband, social security by husband and psychological and emotional support by the family. Due to familiar bond there is no emotional isolation in the life of *dalit* women. Emotional isolation makes people depressed and compel them to commit suicide. So marriage bond give emotional support and protect the life of woman also. Due to re-marriage husband gives economical protection to his wife, she gets rights in husband property also. So due to financial support *dalit* women do not go for wage earning etc.

In Muslims practice temporary marriage (*muta*) but Hindus do not. Hindus do not observe *iddat* for contracting marriages. Lastly, Hindus look down upon the widow re-marriage but Muslims do not.

In Muslims re-marriage is socially accepted because in their religion it is considered that in such a great world, there may be a mistake is selection of life partners. So instead of conflicts and violence in life they give permission for divorce for easily and again give a chance of re-marriage to have a peaceful comfortable life, with social security and economic support. Social acceptance of re-marriage in Christian also in all over the world.

Social Impact

Family, which is a basic unit for society, in which child birth, child-rearing, economic support, social security, emotional support etc. takes place. For a deserted women social security economic security, psychological security is needed. If she has children then security of children in all aspects of life is needed. So to get all positive aspects of life, it is better to get remarry instead of isolated life in the society. In *dalit* society re-marriage is socially accepted which is beneficial for *dalit* women.

In most of cases re-marriage will not have any impact on child support. The new husband is not legally responsible for the children. The children are the responsibility of their parents. The court will base child support on the income of the parents. This often raises problems when the children's mother marries a new husband who is wealthy. The father may have a tight budget and paying child support is a financial hardship. Meanwhile, the ex-wife and children are living an affluent life. Because the children are well taken care of by the mother and step-father the father feels his support is not necessary, at least not at the level he has been paying. The burden for this type of adjustment is very high and the reduction will not usually be granted. This situation changes dramatically if the mother's new husband adopts the minor children. In this scenario the step-father becomes a legal father to the children and is now required to provide for them. The natural father is no longer responsible for ongoing support of the children. There are two things to keep in mind about adoption. First, the adoptive father will be responsible for future support but the biological father will be responsible for any arrears which accumulated prior to the adoption. Second, and more importantly, if the children are adopted the biological father loses his legal standing and is no longer entitled to parenting time with the children.

In United States, with a divorce rate of about 50 per cent, re-marriages add to the complexity of these interactions, because step children and step parents may be involved as well as siblings, which often include half-siblings and step siblings.

Impact of Re-marriage with Family and Child Support

There has also been an increase in the number of re-marriages in which the wife, the husband, or both have offspring from a previous marriage, the number of cohabiting couples who become parents, and the number of gay and Lesbian couples with children (either adopted or the offspring of one of the partners).

Economic Impact

As popular saying *"Roti, Kapra aur Makan"* indicates the needs of human being without bread survival is quite impossible. If there is earning of breads then shelter is needed, of course – it is house i.e. *makan*.

All emotions, feelings are on second step, first is food for survival, for food money is needed. So economic factor is the most important factor for survival. To get financial support, if *dalit* women remarry it is better to have bread, shelter etc. instead of starvation or death. So re-marriage for economic purpose is a good sign in *dalit* society i.e. socially accepted ritual.

Women may get several economical benefits such as survivor's benefits, retirement benefits, and other long term benefits such as household property, land, merchandise etc. Economic support give a stable status in the society to a *dalit* women.

But re-marriage after age 60 (or age 50 if you are disabled) will not prevent one from getting benefit payments based on former spouse's work. And at age 62 or older, one may get benefits based on her new spouse's work, if those benefits would be higher.

Remarry after one reaches 60 will continue to qualify for benefits on deceased spouse's social security record.

However, if current spouse is a social security beneficiary, he/she may want to apply for a wife's or husband's benefit on his or her record if it would be larger than one's widow's or widower's benefit. One cannot get both.

If one's step-mother's new husband is also getting social security, she can apply to receive the wife's benefit of his social security if it would be higher than what she's getting now. Otherwise, she's better off sticking with the benefit she's getting now.

Regardless, she can't lose her existing benefit because she's already turned 62, even though she's re-married.

Psychological Impact

Society is a web of social relationship and man is a social animal.

Family is a universally accepted institution. If is a primary group of society in which two people share their emotions, feelings, love, affection etc. with each other. Loneliness creates manifestation of abnormal behaviour. Anxiety, hypertension, suicidal tendencies can be easily found in lonely persons. To avoid such type of health hazards, it is better to have companion to make a company in the form of family. Divorced women, widow or deserted women face severe psychological problems due to isolation. Even their children, if they have, also face severe psychological stress/ problems due to isolation.

So to check mate emotional problems or psychological stresses, it is better to remarry, as *dalit* women do in their life. As popular saying "Love is a great heeler". It is better to share emotions and feelings etc. in the form of wedlock.

Advantages of Re-marriage

Loneliness is accompanied by negative affect including feeling of depression, anxiety, unhappiness and dissatisfaction associated with pessimism, self blame and shyness etc.

To counter the negative affect of loneliness, it is better to has a companion in the form of wedlock i.e. re-marriage.

Compared to single individuals, those who are married consistently report being happier and healthier. In Norway, married people, compared to those who are single, report a greater sense of well-being and have a lower suicide rate – at least until they reach their late thirties, after that, the advantage of being re-married begin to disappear.

Despite the shattered hopes of living happily ever after and despite the emotional pain of a marital breakup, it is interesting to note that most divorced individuals marry again. In fact half of all marriages is the U.S. are re-marriages for one or both partners. The desire for future love and happiness in a relationship seems to have a greater influence on behaviors than the negative interactions with a former spouse.

Promoting Factors of Re-marriage in *Dalit* Castes

A definition of successful marriage that is supported by social science evidence: namely, a long lasting union in which both spouses express mutual satisfaction with their relationship; hold similar values, attitudes and beliefs; are sexually faithful to each other; have adequate resources to care for each other and their children; share a common commitment to the well-being of their children; live together peaceably without persistent conflict, abuse or violence; are embedded within a supportive social network of family, friends and community; and are sustained by the larger society's support for marriage as the favoured institution for sex, procreation and parenthood.

The turbulent market economy, the frazzled pace of daily life and the shallow relationships in a mobile society hardly after a hospitable climate for marriage. And a popular culture that pushes images of sex without strings and relationships without rings hardly reflects the desires of most people for an enduring and satisfying marriage. Indeed, a happy and lasting marriage ranks as one of the most highly prized and hardest-to-achieve accomplishments in contemporary life.

Objectives

1. To assess the socio-economic status of *dalit* castes
2. To know the views of the respondents regarding re-marriage
3. To study the impact of sociological, economic and psychological status of *dalit* women regarding re-marriage.
4. To suggests ways to remove social evils regarding re-marriage.

Justification of the Study

In India among Brahmin and Vaishyas, widows do not remarry, marriage by widows of these castes is considered improper, immoral and irreligious. In short, among Hindu marriage is compulsory. It is a sacrament an indestructible and secret union. Second marriage especially for women are abhorred. Widows and divorcee is not viewed similarly by some other castes. So among them and especially in *dalit* castes. Some widows and divorcee do marry again, a second marriage by a widow and divorcee may be due to economic or social reasons.

Raja Ram Mohan Roy, Ishwar Chandra Vidyasagar, Mahatma Gandhi and Dr. B.R. Ambedkar favoured widow re-marriage. The Hindu Widows Re-marriage Act, 1856 removed all legal obstacles to the marriage of Hindu widows. The object was to promote good moral and public welfare.

Re-marriage is socially acceptable in *dalit* castes. Even a person having her own children is accepted by re-marriage. Re-marriage give strength to a person because stress of life either, it is due to marital conflicts or any reason is always harmful for a human being. So passing life in isolation or with feeling of burden of life it is better to have a companion as wife for happiness of life. Re-marriage make to people socially, economically, psychologically more secure. It is also good for development of country because the Pt. Jawaharlal Nehru said "You can tell the condition of a nation by looking at the status of its women". This is absolutely true. So we should promotes to other caste for re-marriage, because it is not a social evil in present scenario.

CHAPTER 2

Review of Literature

The review of literature is the basis of most of the research.

"The literature in any field forms the foundation upon which all future work is built".

Review of related literature of the study has become an established practice of all research reports but this should not be taken as mere practice or tradition in writing research process. Briefly it may be pointed out that review of related literature gives an insight into the problem. The important aspect of this tradition is that the researcher comes to know about the present position of the problem and also its explored and unexplored aspects of her problem. It was in view of these considerations that the investigator shifted the pages of journals, abstracts and internet, so that the different aspect of problem may be elaborated.

Easterlin (1999) offers an additional theory of marriage in his "relative income hypothesis". He concluded that men are the primary bread-winners and believes women's labour supply to be determined by the ability of the man to meet the couple's economic needs, the general premise of the theory is applicable.

U.N. Division for the Advancement of Women (2000), Fuller (1965) widow re-marriage may be forbidden in the higher castes and re-marriage, where permitted, may be restricted to a family member. Further, a widow, upon remarriage, may be required to relinquish custody of her children as well as any property rights she may have. If she keeps her children with her, she may fear they would be ill-treated in a second marriage. Indian widows are often regarded as "evil eyes" the purveyors of ill fortune and unwanted burdens on poor families.

U.N. Division for the Advancement of Women (2000) India is perhaps the only country where widowhood, in addition to being a personal status, exists as a social institution. Widow's deprivation and stigmatization are exacerbated by ritual and religious symbolism. Indian society, similar to all patriarchal societies, confers social status on a women through a man. Hence, in the absence of a man, she herself becomes a non-entity, ultimately suffering a social death. Sati (widow burning) is the ultimate manifestation of this belief.

Bruce (2005), Daman (2007), U.N. Division for the Advancement of Women (2000) younger widows are forced into prostitution, and older ones are left to beg and chant for alms from pilgrims and tourists. Older widows may have lived the greater part of their lives in these temples, having been brought there as child widows many years before. The ordeals of the temple widows and the occasional *sati* are publicised in the international press. But, the day-to-day suffering of Indian widows, who are emotionally, physically and sexually abused by relatives, or who migrate to cities to live on the streets and beg, remains largely hidden.

U.N. Division for the Advancement of Women (2000) widows, through poor nutrition, inadequate shelter, lack of access to health care and vulnerability to violence, are very likely to suffer not only physical ill health but stress and chronic depression as well widow may be victims of rape. This is further compounded by the fact that widows, in common with many women, are very often unaware of their rights, and encounter insuperable barriers to accessing justice system, such as illiteracy, expenses and threats of violence *(Ibid)*.

David Popenoe and Barbara Dafoe Whitehead (2000) say that a prolonged period of sexually active single hood may also encourage a marriage – oversethos among men. By living with a girlfriend, men can get many of the benefits of marriage without making a commitment to marriage. Also, some men regard marriage as "hard work" whereas the single life promises "fun and freedom". Given this view of marriage, they seek to prolong the "fun and freedom" of the single life as long as they can.

Bumpass et al. criticized the overwhelming attention paid by social scientists to women's economic independence in explaining recent demographic trends. The empirical support for economic – independence, explanation of marriage behaviour is mixed.

Rosenfield, et al. (2000) critics have argued that gender difference in distress among the married and the unmarried may reflect selection factors whereby emotionally healthy men are more likely to select into marriage and emotionally healthy women are more likely to select out of marriage, in the first place.

Waite and Gallagher (2000) concluded that the mental health benefits of marriage currently apply equally to women and men. However, once again, because most of these studies include emotional problems common among males, they also provide an incomplete picture of the relationship among gender, marital status and mental health.

Parry et al. (2000) for provocative discussion of biological (i.e. hormonal and genetic) influences on mood disorders and substance abuse among females and males. It is, of course, entirely possible that women's higher levels of depression and men's greater alcohol abuse not only reflect gender – linked emotional socialization, but also reflect biological differences that predispose males and females to manifest distress with different types of mental health problems.

Simon and Kanellokos (2001) revealed a consequence of gender linked emotional socialization is that females learn to express distress through internalizing emotional problem, such as depression, while males learn to express distress vis-à-vis externalizing emotional problems, such as substance abuse and females manifest distress with different type of emotional problems, role arguments are most useful for explaining differences in mental health among men and women.

Popenoe and Whitehead (2001) present as one measure of this trend, consider the results of a 2001 national survey of single and married young adults ages 20-29. Only 16 per cent agree that the main purpose of marriage is to have children, while 62 per cent agree that while it may not be ideal. It's okay for an adult woman to have a child on her own if she has not found the right man to marry. More than four out of ten describe adults who choose to raise a child out of wedlock as "doing their own thing". Among the sample's singles, less than half (42%) agree that it is important to find a spouse who shares their own religious faith.

Popenoe and Whitehead (2001) while marriage is losing much of its public and institutional character, it is gaining popularity as a "soulmate" relationship – an intensely private couple relationship whose main purpose is to promote the psychological well-being and emotional satisfaction of each adult. Over eighty per cent of all young women, married and single, agree that "it is more important to them to have a husband who can communicate about his deepest feelings than to have a husband who makes a good living."

Daniel T. Lichter and *John H. Cragnon (2001)* non marital childbearing negatively affects a women's chance of forming a successful marriage in the future. Once a woman has had a child outside of marriage, her chances of marrying drop dramatically. According to one recent study, that chance is almost 40 per cent lower for those who had a first child outside of marriage and 51 per cent for women who do not marry the biological father within six months of birth. By age 35, only 70 per cent of all unwed mothers are married compared to 88 per cent of those who have not a child.

Gary Becker's (2001) stated that women's increasing economic independence during this period is a common explanation for the decline in first marriage rates. Women's rising income is translated into reduced economic dependence on a spouse, causing women to feel less economic incentive to marry.

Linda J. Waite et al. (2002), there is some evidence that marriages that are unhappy at one point can become happy at a later point in time. One recent large scale study indicates that 86 per cent of people who said they were unhappily married in the late 1980s but stayed in the marriage indicated that they were happier when they were interviewed five years later. Indeed, three-fifth's of the formerly unhappily married couples rated their marriages as either "very happy" or "quite happy".

Popenoe, David (2002), marrying as a teen is the highest known risk factor for divorce. Teenagers who marry are two to three times more likely to have unhappy marriages and to divorce than people who marry in their twenties.

Edin and Kafalas (2002), some sociologist have attributed the decline of high paying low skill jobs to a shortage of "marriageable men" especially among African – American men in the inner city. Other scholars contend that the loss of high paying low skills jobs only partially explains the retreat from marriage. They also point to men's sexual attitudes and behaviors particularly high levels of infidelity, promiscuity and paternal irresponsibility – as a key reason why women reject such men as unsuitable marriage partners.

Cherlin, Andrew J. (2002) says that during the recent decades of high divorce and rising cohabitation the valuation of marriage has remained remarkable persistent. The vast majority of men and women seek lasting marriage as a personal life goal. Indeed the belief in marriage is stronger in the U.S. than in most other developed countries, in the world values surveys conducted between 1999 and 2001 only 10 per cent of Americans agreed with the statement "marriage is an out-dated institution" compared to 22 per cent of Canadians, 26 per cent of British and 36 per cent of the French.

Edin and Kefalas (2002) postponing marriage until older ages exposes sexually active young single adults to the risks of multiple failed relationship, cohabitation, and unwed parenthood. Sexual infidelity after figures in these broken relationship. As a result women who have experienced several breakups in their late teens and early twenties have a hard time trusting the "next guy who comes along". Low-income women are at high risk for this kind of gender mistrust and a estrangement.

Thara (2002) says that several reasons have been cited for opting out of marriages these days – increasing violence, cruelty, character assassination, alcoholism, problems of adjustment especially in a joint family, rowing individualism of the wrong type, extra-marital affairs and the undesirable impact of the outside world in terms of falling values and lack of role models.

Lee (2002) says that the problem is further increased by dismal rates of re-marriage among women in developing states. Re-marriage rates are mostly lower for women because there are very few available men in the appropriate age ranges. This is exacerbated by the fact that older widowed men who remarry frequently marry younger women, while marriage of older women to younger men are much less common (*Ibid*). Nonetheless, re-marriage is uncommon among widowed individuals, particularly when they are widowed late in life (Ibid).

Chiappori, Pierre – et al. (2003) shows that the production of children is a major reason for marriage. However, investment in children often creates ex-post differences between otherwise identical men and women. The mother is the one who gives birth and it is generally considered to be more capable of taking care of the children, at least initially. This basic difference may have large economic consequences.

Amato, Poul R. and Stacy J. Rogers (2003) according to the well established role of marital homogamy, the more similar people are in age, education, religion and race, the more likely they are to have a successful marriage. However, fewer Americans today are entering homogamous marriages. The proportion of interracial and interethnic marriages has increased among all groups in the society. This is a matter of concern because people in heterogamous marriage report less marital happiness and greater proneness to divorce. Overall, the increase in marital heterogamy may be one reason for lower levels of marital quality, satisfaction and duration.

Edin and Kefalas, (2002) in the minds of young people today, marriage is reserved for couples who are able to afford a "decent" wedding as well as a house with furniture, a nice care or two, and an occasional vacation or dinner out. Until young adults are able to afford these material goods, they are putting off marriage.

Teachman, Jay (2003) many young people believe that cohabitation will improve their chances for having a lasting marriage, there is no evidence to support that belief. On the contrary, a substantial body of evidence suggests that cohabiting couples are more likely to breakup after marriage than those who do not live together before marriage.

Twenge, Jean M. et al. (2003), the exacting emotional requirements are likely to make marriages unhappier and potentially more fragile. When married couples cannot look to larger institutional forces, such as religion, law or social norms, to sustain their union, they bear the burden of maintaining a high quality marriage on their own. This is especially true for parents who have full-time jobs outside the home. This may explain why parents now report significantly lower marital satisfaction than non parents.

Aseltine and Kessler (2003) say that women are more distressed by marital loss. The handful of studies that have assessed the effects of marital gain indicate that marriage reduces the distress of men and women, but that there are no sex differences in the emotional benefits of marriage.

Scannell (2003) says that people respond differently to loss and overcome grief in their own time. Frequently, the most difficult time for new widows is after the funeral. Young widows often have no peer group. Compared to older widows, they are generally less prepared emotionally and practically to cope with the loss. Widowhood often causes financial stress because a major income source is lost with the death of a husband.

Popenoe, David (2004) says that it is increasingly common for one or both married individuals to come from divorced parent families. According to one study, the divorce risk nearly tripled if both individuals come from a broken home; if the wife alone had experienced parental divorce, however, the increased risk was significantly reduced.

Wilcox, W. Bradford and Steven L. Knock (2004) shared religious observance promotes greater emotional investment in marriage by man. This is an important finding because today's wives evaluate marital quality largely on the basis of emotional well-being. According to one recent study, husbands' emotional investment in the marriage – meaning the high quality time men spend with their wives and the love and affection they show to their wives – is the most *crucial* determinant of women's marital satisfaction.

Wolf, Douglas A. (2004) cross-national studies of cultural trends point to the pervasive effects of a modern form of individualism that places high value on individual expressiveness, privacy, autonomy, and freedom from institutional controls over sex and family life. To a large degree, the value of personal freedom in private life overrides concerns for child well-being, family stability, and kin loyalty. Even economic self-interest takes a back seat to the quest for independent selfhood. People will sacrifice a degree of economic well-being – even, in the extreme, cause themselves to be classified as poor to achieve the autonomy and privacy that accompany independent living.

Laomann, Edward O. and *John H. Gagnon (2004)* present a report in non-marital six and unwed child-bearing phase which shows that men and women who are virgins at marriage have dramatically more stable marriages than those who have non-marital sex. This is largely due to the fact that those who obtain from non marital sex are also more likely to be religious and to have a strong commitment to lifelong marriage.

Whitehead, Barbara Dofoe (2004) speaks that since its peak in the early 1980s, the divorce rate has continued to drop. It has fallen from a high of 22.6 per 1000 married women in 1980 to 17.7 per 1000 married women in 2004. However, the decline in the divorce rate has done little to erase the cultural legacy of divorce. The widespread social experience of divorce has led to attitudes and behaviour that have now taken on a life and momentum of their own. Indeed, it could be argued that the habit of mind created by a culture of divorce have had more harmful effects on marriage than divorce itself.

Mirani, Haroon (2004) say that with killing, torture, rapes, molestations, disappearances and detentions becoming the order of the day in Kashmir, psychiatric disorders have seen a sharp increase post 1989. In 1989, about 1,700 patients visited the valley's lone psychiatric hospital and by the year 2003. The number had gone up to 48,000. Before the onset of the armed struggle, certain disorders that were not known to Kashmiris starts showing a significant presence amongst the civilian population. The Post-Traumatic Stress

Disorder (PSTD), one of the psychiatric diseases, which was completely unrecognized before 1990 has witnessed a major upsurge. Major Depressive Disorder (MDO) follows this. There are other mental diseases like bipolar disorder, panic, phobia, general anxiety and sleep disorders that have also shown four fold increase as told by Dr. Arshad of the Psychiatric Diseases Hospital in Srinagar. Dr. Mishtaq Marghoob, a leading psychiatrist of the Vally states that women bear the brunt of every tragedy. They have to support the family after the death of their husbands, fathers, sons or brothers. Dr. Arshad further adds that women form a major part of the patients who are suffering from PSTD (almost 50 %). For women whose husbands have died, psychotherapy has failed to produce desired results.

Kessler and McRac (2004) say that marriage is beneficial for men's mental health and detrimental for women's, research consistently indicates that marriage is associated with enhanced mental health for men and women. Studies that have focused on marital status differences in well-being among men and among women (i.e., marital status within gender analysis) show that regardless of gender, married people enjoy better mental health than, unmarried (including newer and formerly remarried persons).

Oppenheimer (2004) concluded that impact of transition to a stable work role on the timing of first marriage, her theory has important implication for re-marriage. Because jobs held in young adulthood may have little relation to later occupational success, early occupational status may be considered on uncertain predictor for first marriage.

Chiappori, Pierre-Andre and Yoram Weiss (2005) revealed that in modern marriage market display increasing turnover, with less marriage but more divorce and re-marriage. As a consequence, a large number of children live in single parent and step parent household.

Bramlett, Matthew and William D. Mosher (2005) there is no significant difference between white non-Hispanic women and Hispanic women in the stability of first marriage. Available data suggest that first marriages of Asian women are more stable than among any other group.

Popenoe, David and Barbara Dafoe Whitehead (2005) a robust body of social science evidence points to the positive economic, health and social benefits of long-lasting marriage for men, women and children. Yet the benefits and advantages of marriage are not as broadly distributed or widely shared as they once were. In recent decades there has been a dramatic change in marrying behaviour. Today as compared to thirty years ago, Americans are more likely to live together before and after marriage, to postpone marriage until older ages, to divorce more and to remarry less, and never to marry at all. At any given age, individuals are less likely to be, or have ever been, married. The marriage rate reflects these changes. Since 1970, the marriage rate has fallen by nearly fifty per cent, from 76.5 per 1000 unmarried women to 39.9 per 1000 unmarried women in 2004.

Sciences (2005) says Blacks are the least likely to marry to stay married, and to remarry. They are the most likely to cohabit, to divorce and to become unwed parents. This gap shows up in attitudes among the young as well. According to the 2002 findings in the National Survey of Family Growth, African American teenage boys are less likely to favour marriage and more likely to approve of divorce than either Hispanic or non-Hispanic white teen boys.

Amato, Paul R. (2005) individuals who grow in on married parent family are more likely to marry and to stay married than individuals whose families were broken by divorce or whose parents never married. Compared to individuals from disrupted family backgrounds, individuals who grew up with both married parents are more likely to have a positive experience of a marriage, to have a commitment to life long marriage, to have mothers who are more positive about marriage and less permissive of divorce, and to have greater emotional security and trust in their own future marriages.

Radloff, Lenore S. (2005) indicates that women report more mental health problems than men, irrespective of marital status. Studies that have focused on gender differences in psychological well being among the married and among the remarried (i.e. gender within marital status analyses) find that women report greater distress than comparable men in all marital status categories.

Amato et al. (2005) religious teachings offers strong normative support for marriage and for the norm of marital performance. Belief in marital performance is associated with higher levels of marital quality for both men and women. When couples see marriage as a lifting commitment, they tend to make high personal investments of time, attention and affection in their relationship with the expectation that they will mutually benefit over the long term. They are less likely to indulge in day-by-day calculations of who is doing more and who is getting a better "deal" a habit of mind that can lead to resentment, conflict and a withdrawal of emotional investment.

Stanley, S.M. et al. (2005) researchers hypothesize, may persist after marriage. Cohabiting couples may "slide" into marriage rather than "decide" to marry. In other words, they may fail to undergo the transition from the contingent commitment of a cohabiting partnership to the permanent commitment of marriage. By carrying a "cohabiting mindset" into marriage, they are then at greater risk for divorce. The loss of time and opportunity can be especially hazardous for women who want to marry and have children before they get to the age where they are at risk for infertility problems.

Popenoe and Whitehead (2005), the proportion of cohabiting mothers who eventually marry the father of their children has declined from 57 to 44 per cent in the decade between 1987-97. Nor are these cohabiting parent household as stable as married parent household. At the five year mark, half of cohabiting couples with children will have broken up compared to 15 per cent of married parents. Children who live in cohabiting household with their biological mother and an unrelated male partner face a high risk of sexual abuse and physical violence.

Popenoe, David and Barbara Dafoe Whitehead (2005) in recent decades, living together has shifted form a stigmatized and marginal practice to a socially acceptable and main stream practice for opposite sex couples. Between 1960 and 2004, the number of unmarried couples increased from less than 500,000 to more than five million. Over half of all first marriages are now preceded by a living together relationship. Cohabiting partnerships are highly unstable. Most break up within a year, either by ending altogether or converting to marriage.

Marriage and Family (2005) this pervasive form of individualism has negatively affected marriage and family life in very different kinds of advanced western societies. As sociologist David Popenoe points out, both the highly religious United States and the highly secular Sweden have experienced high levels of family breakdown over roughly the same time period. In the U.S. 63 per cent of children under 18 live with their own biological parents, down from 58 per cent as recently as 1970 and now the lowest percentage among all western industrialized nations, Sweden, at 73 per cent, is the second lowest.

See discussion of gender differences in Whitehead (2005) these gendered views of cohabitation may help explain why some cohabiting men are surprised, annoyed or mystified when their live in girlfriend brings up the subject of marriage and why cohabiting men regard talk of future marriage as an unwanted "pressure". On the other sides it is also why some cohabiting women feel cruelly deceived when their live in boy friends back of marriage.

Bianchi and Spain (2006) concluded that the family income of women who do not remarry is 70 per cent of its pre-separation level within the first year after separation or divorce and only 71 per cent of its previous level five years after dissolution.

Bill I (2006) presented that thousands of widows are disowned by their relatives and thrown out of their homes in the context of land and inheritance disputes. Their options, given a lack of education and training, are mostly limited to becoming exploited, unregulated, domestic labourers (often as house slaves within the husband's family) or turning to begging or prostitution.

James, Sweet and Larry Bumpass (2007) revealed that in the era of high divorce rates and postponement of the first marriage, re-marriage has become on increasingly important event in American family life. One half of are marriage have involved at least one previous married partner. While re-marriage fulfills needs for love and companionship, instrumental benefits of re-marriage may also be high.

Amato, Poul R. and Alan Booth (2007) the emphasis on more subjective and adult centered measures of marital well being also contributes to the persistently high rate of parental divorce. As many as two third of the parental divorces in recent years occurs, not because of domestic violence, drug addition or other destructive behaviours, but because of "softer" forms of psychological distress and unhappiness.

Wadhwa, Soma (2007) has described how, during a great festival at the *Sati* temple in Jhunjhunu, a slightly confused fresh tourist caused tremendous shock by asking whether women in India who wanted to commit *Sati* had to come to this temple to do so. One of the worshippers told him "India is a progressive country". Women are not burnt here. They are respected. To us they are mothers, devis, goddesses. We worship them". Soma Wadwas's comment was: "Do women want to be worshipped? Or, would they rather have equal rights?"

Fasoranti et al. (2007) ironically, the disorganization and trauma that follow the death of a spouse seem to be greater in women than in men, whenever either looses their spouse. Widowhood presents a myriad of economic, social and psychological problems, particularly in the first year so after the death of the spouse. A major problem for both sexes is economic hardship. When the husband was the principal breadwinner, his widow is now deprived of his income and the nucleus of the family is destroyed.

Fasoranti et al. (2007) says that the another problem associated with widowhood is loneliness. Many widows live by themselves. They suffer the fear of being alone and loss of self-esteem as women, in addition to the many practical problems related to living alone. They feel the loss of personal contact and human association, therefore, they tend to withdraw and become unresponsive.

Patterson, Orlando (2008) men and women who are college educated are more likely to marry, to stay married and to report satisfaction in marriage than people with lower levels of educational attainment. Also college-educated individuals are more likely to marry other college-educate individuals in the future, however, it may become more difficult for college educated women to find similarly well educated men it more women than men continue to earn college degrees.

U.S. Bureau of the Census (2008) despite the decline in re-marriage rates, re-marriages constitute an increasing proportion of all marriage both because of the increasing pools of divorced individuals at risk of re-marriage and the trend toward delayed first marriage.

Simon, Robin W. (2008) revealed that Gove introduced his sex role theory of mental illness, which attributes women's higher rates of psychological distress to their soles in society. Central to his hypothesis in that marriage is emotionally advantageous for men and disadvantageous for women.

Rose (2008) using data from the 1980 census, we find that the rate of marital dissolution is 4 per cent higher for women whose firstborn child is a girl. Since firstborn sex is essentially random, we can construct a credible instrument for divorce in the population of women with at least one child born during her first marriage.

Ananat and Michaels (2008) report similar estimates for the relationship between the sex of the first born child and the probability of marital dissolution using the 1980 census. As was previously observed, cross-sectional OLS comparisons of standardized (person-adjusted) household income and poverty rates among ever-and-never-divorced women indicates a substantial economic disadvantage for ever divorced women.

Ruggles and Sobek (2008) says that well suited for an analysis of marital instability and the economic well being of women because it contains information on marital history and indicators of economic status for a large and representative sample of women. Which makes the dating of the first marriage relative to the first birth impossible. Because our empirical strategy relies an identifying the sex of the first child born during the first marriage.

Burnard (2009) argued that marriage is emotionally advantageous for men and disadvantageous to women, which she attributed to gender inequality in power and authority, in both the family and society. While feminist scholars continue to stress the linkages between families and wider system of male domination for understanding gender inequality in a variety of contexts.

Goldstein (2009) they become more vocal and are willing to sacrifice their family of for the sake of independence. Although it is not good sign for the society as a whole, which has to depend on family structure, it is inevitable. However, it would be wrong to even hint that only women are responsible for this alarming trend. Many a times continuing in an abusive and unsatisfying marriage has had grater effect on the psyche of spouses and children rather than opting to be parted amicably or through court.

Crove et al. (2009) in contrast, other argue that traditional gender roles (e.g. the unequal distribution of unpaid household work) would predict single women to be better off than single men.

CHAPTER 3

Profile of the Study Area

Prior to discuss the findings of the study on "Advantages of re-marriage in Dalit castes", it is essential to sketch briefly the salient features.

District Kanpur

Kanpur is said to be the corruption of Kanhaiyapur or Kanhpur, which was an unimportant village till its first contact with the British. According to a local tradition, the name of Kanhpur Kohna owes its origin to Hindu Singh, Raja of Sachendi, who came here about 1750, to *bathe* in the holy river, the Ganga and established a village, which he (possibly) named Kanhpur, the name becoming changed to Kanpur in the course of time.

Location

The district of Kanpur occupies the north-western part of the Allahabad division and belongs to the tract known as the lower doab (which comprises the eastern extremity of the strip of country lying between the Ganga and the Yamuna rivers). In shape, it is an irregular quadrilateral and lies between the parallel of 25°26' and 26°58' north latitude and 70°31' and 80°34' east longitude. To the north-east, beyond the Ganga, the deep stream of which forms the boundary of the district, lie the districts of Hardoi and Unnao, while to the south, across the Yamuna, are the districts of Hamirpur and Jalaun. On the south-east, the boundary marches with that of Bindki (a tahsil of Fatehpur) and to the west and north-west are the Auraiya and Bidhuna tahsils of district Auraiya and that of Kannauj district.

Area

According to the Central Statistical Organization, the district had an area of 3015 Sq.km (Census, 2001) with 1040 Sq.km area covered under Kanpur, district, from which four zones were selected for the present study.

Population

According to the census of 2001, the district had a population of 25,51,337 in which 13,74,121 are males and 11,77,216 are females and occupied the 2nd position in the state in respect of population.

Climate

The climate of the district is characterized by a hot summer and general dryness except in the south-west monsoon season. The year may be divided into four seasons. The period from March to about the middle of June is the summer season, which is followed by the south-west monsoon season which lasts till about the end of September, October and the first half of November forms the post-monsoon or transition period. The cold season spreads from about the middle of November to February.

Rainfall

Records in rainfall in the district are available for 8 stations for periods ranging from 51 to 97 years. The average annual rainfall in the district is 778.9 mm (30.67"). The rainfall in the district varies from 642.3 mm (25.29") at Narwal to 884.8

mm (34.83") at Kanpur. About 89 per cent of the annual rainfall is received during the monsoon months (June to September). August being the rainiest month. The variation in the annual rainfall from year to year as appreciable. In the fifty-year period, 1901 to 1950, the highest rainfall, which was 155 per cent of the normal, occurred in 1904. The lowest annual rainfall, 43 per cent of the normal, occurred in 1981. In this fifty-year period, the annual rainfall in the district was less than 80 per cent of the normal in 12 years, none of which were consecutive.

Temperature

There is a meteorological observatory at Kanpur and the record of this observatory may be taken as representative of the climatic conditions prevailing in the district in general. About the beginning of March there is a rapid rise in temperature. May and the early part of June constitute the hottest part of the year. The mean daily maximum temperature in May is 41.3°C (106°F) or above. Hot dry and dust leaden westerly winds are common in the hot season. Afternoon thunder showers that occur a few times during the summer, bring temporary relief, with the onset of monsoon after the middle of June, the day temperature drops appreciably. Nights continue to be as warm as those during the latter part of the summer. Towards the end of the monsoon (in September and in October) there is a slight increase in the day temperature, but the nights temperatures decrease rapidly. January ion generally the coldest month with the mean daily maximum temperature at 22.3°C (72.1°F) and the mean daily minimum at 78°C (46.0°F). During the cold season, in association with passing western disturbances, cold weaves affect the district and the minimum temperature drops down to about the freezing point of water and frost occurs. The highest maximum and the lowest maximum temperature recorded in the year 1996-97 and 1997-98 were 44.2°C and 0.7°C, respectively.

Humidity

During the monsoon season, the humidity generally exceeds 70 per cent but after that is decreases. The driest part of the year is the summer season when in the afternoon the humidity is less than 30 per cent.

Selected Sample of Kanpur City

Kanpur is a big city. Different slum areas are here. Ten slums were selected in this study. 250 dalit women were selected in this study.

CHAPTER 4

Research Methodology

This chapter deals with the research procedures applied in conducting the present study. For convenience, the research methodology has been discussed under the following three sub-heads :

1. Research design
2. Variables and their operationalization
3. Data gathering procedure and statistical techniques used

1. Research Design

It comprises of the following sub-parts :

(i) Locale of the study

(ii) Selection of the slums

(iii) Sample of respondents

(i) Locale of the Study : The study was undertaken in Kanpur district of Uttar Pradesh.

(ii) Selection of the Slums : Ten slum areas were selected randomly.

(a) 104/334, Sisamau

(b) 104/327-331 Sisamau

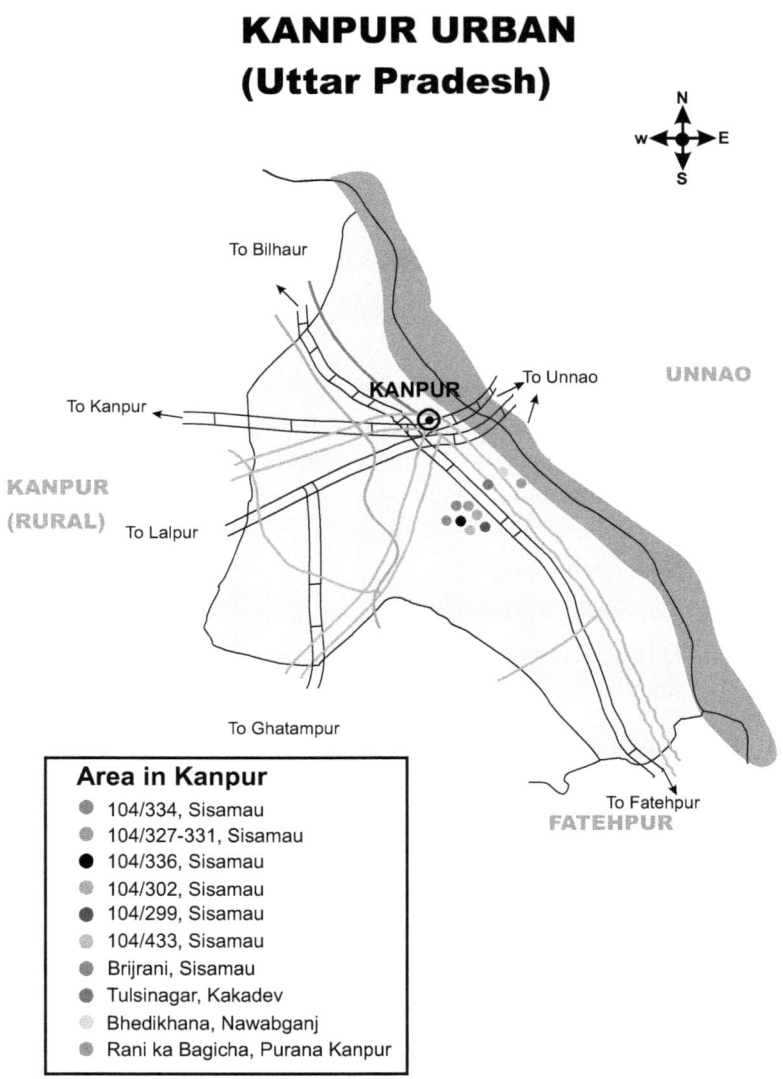

(c) 104/336, Sisamau

(d) 104/302, Sisamau

(e) 104/299, Sisamau

(f) 104/433, Sisamau

(g) Brijrani, Sisamau

(h) Tulsi Nagar, Kakadeo

(i) Bhedikhana, Nawabganj

(j) Rani Ka Bagicha, Purana Kanpur

***(iii)* Sample of respondents :** According to requirement of the study 25 Dalit women were selected form each slums. Thus, total 250 dalit women were selected randomly.

Variables and their Measurements

Considering ability of the variables in accordance with the objectives of the study, dependent and independent variables were included for the present investigation.

***(i)* Independent Variables:** The independent variables which were covered in the study are described as under :

(a) Age : Age was operationalized as number of full years, completed by the respondents at the time of interview. The age of respondents was measured by direct questioning. The respondents were categorized into five age groups and the following scoring pattern was observed

Age-group (years)	Score assigned
20 – 25	1
25 – 30	2
30 – 35	3
35 – 40	4
40 – 45	5

(b) Education : Education refers to the schooling education one has achieved. Educational scoring system followed in socio-economic status scale of Trivedi (1963) with certain modifications.

Level of Education	Score assigned
Illiterate	1
Primary	2
Middle	3
High School	4
Intermediate	5

(c) Caste : Caste refers to the social rank attributed to the respondents in the study. The respondents were classified into sub castes of Dalit category as per following procedure.

Caste	Score assigned
Dhobi	1
Jatav	2
Valmiki	3
Pasi	4
Julaha	5
Ravidasia Sikh	6
Katheria	7

(d) Type of the family : Family composition was scored on the basis of

According of family type	Score assigned
Nuclear family	1
Joint family	2

(e) Size of the family : Family size scored on the basis of

Family size	Score assigned
Up to 4 members	1
4 to 8 members	2
8 and above members	3

(f) Occupation : This was measured on the basis of the scores allotted to different family occupation in the socio-economic status cycle developed by Trivedi (1963).

Occupation	Score assigned
Home servant	1
Daily wages worker	2
Caste occupation	3
House wife	4

(g) Religion : The selected area was having mostly Hindu religion and some are Muslim, Sikh and Christian. The following scoring pattern was adopted.

Religion	Score assigned
Hindu	1
Muslim	2
Sikh	3
Christian	4

(h) Marital status : Marital status was scored on the basis.

Marital status	Score assigned
Married	1
Divorcee	2
Re-married	3
Widow	4

(i) Monthly income : The position of an individual or a family occupies with reference to the prevailing standards of cultural possession, monthly income, material possession etc. The following scoring pattern was adopted –

Marital status	Score assigned
Up to Rs. 1,500	1
Rs. 1,500 to Rs. 3,000	2
Rs. 3,000 to Rs. 4,500	3
Rs. 4,500 to Rs. 6,000	4
Rs. 6,000 and above	5

(ii) Dependent variables :

(a) Advantage : Any condition, circumstance, opportunity, or means particularly favourable to success, or to any desired end; benefit; is called advantage.

(b) Caste : A ranked group in which membership is determined at birth and marriage is restricted to members of one's own group.

(c) Marriage : Marriage is considered a lifelong partnership. It is the rock on which the family is built and which in turn, is the foundation of society. Basically marriage is a social and legal contract. Frequently it has very little to do with love or any other emotions. Tradition, culture, religion, caste and community pressure, all play an important part in the institution of marriage.

(d) Re-marriage : The act of marrying again or a second or repeated marriage is called re-marriage.

(e) View : Mode of looking at anything; manner of apprehension; conception, opinion; judgment; as, to state one's views of the policy which ought to be pursued which is known as view.

(f) Status : The relative position or standing of things or especially persons in a society, which is known as status.

(g) Social evil : In the smallest unit, social evil exists when a person's behaviour causes harm to another. One should be responsible for one's own existence, while respecting the boundary of others. In this way, if he doesn't harm anyone,

he is free to do whatever he wants which is known as social evil.

(iii) Data gathering procedure and statistical techniques used : The necessary evidences were collected in line with the objectives of the study. The total samples of 250 Dalit women were individually approached by the researcher. By contacting each respondent personally the Dalit women were interviewed with the help of instrument developed in advance and presented over a sample of 50 Dalit women respectively which were other than those included in the final sample of respondents.

Keeping in view the convenience of the female respondents several visits were made for the collection of the data during the course of investigation and wherever possible suitable cross – checking was done.

Period of Investigation

The data collection was initiated from October 2008 to January 2009.

Statistical Techniques

The following statistical techniques have been applied in the analysis of data.

1. Percentage : Single comparisons were made on the basis of the percentage, for drawing percentages, the frequency of a particular cell was multiplied by 100 and divided by total number of respondents in that particular category to which they belonged.

$$Percentage = \frac{\text{The sum of all the responses}}{\text{Total number of all the responses}} \times 100$$

2. Weighted mean : It is average which is calculated on the basis and coding. If $X_1, X_2, X_3, \ldots X_n$, are the codes and $W_1 + W_2 + W_3 \ldots W_n$ are their respective weights, then :

$$\text{Weighted mean} = \frac{W_1X_1 + W_2X_2 + W_3X_3 + \ldots W_nX_n}{W_1 + W_2 + W_3 \ldots W_n}$$

$$= \sum_{i=1}^{n} \frac{W_1X_1}{W_1}$$

3. Correlation coefficient : Karl Pearson has given a coefficient of correlation for the measurement of linear relationship, which exists between two variables. If X and Y are two variables and if $E(X, Y) \neq 0$ then correlation coefficient (r) is

$$r = \frac{\text{Cov.}(X,Y)}{\sqrt{\text{Var.}(X), \text{Var.}(Y)}}$$

or

$$= \frac{\Sigma xy}{\sqrt{\Sigma x^2 \cdot \Sigma y^2}}$$

where

$$\Sigma xy = \left[\Sigma XY - \frac{\Sigma X \Sigma Y}{n}\right]$$

$$\Sigma x^2 = \left[\Sigma X^2 - \frac{(\Sigma X)^2}{n}\right]$$

$$\Sigma y^2 = \left[\Sigma Y^2 - \frac{(\Sigma Y)^2}{n}\right]$$

and n = Sample size

Here, one variable is dependent on other. For testing the significance of correlation coefficient (r), t test is applied. Degree of lack of relationship or coefficient of alienation is measured as –

$$K = \sqrt{1 - r^2}$$

4. Chi-square test : In order to test the independence of two attributes a Chi-square test was applied as :

$$\chi^2 = \sum_{i=1}^{n} \frac{(O_i - E_i)^2}{E_i}$$

Where,

O_i = Observed frequency of ith cell

E_i = Expected frequency of ith cell

In rxc contingency table, χ^2 value is compared at $(r-1) \times (c-1)$ degree of freedom with theoretical value of χ^2 at 5 per cent level of significance.

CHAPTER 5

Findings and Discussion

The empirical results and its discussion have been presented in this chapter. For the purpose of convenience, the presentation has been sub-divided under the following sections, as per the objectives of the study set forth.

I. Socio-economic status of *dalit* castes.

II. The views of the respondents regarding re-marriage.

III. The impact of sociological, economical and psychological status of *dalit* women regarding re-marriage.

IV. Remove social evils regarding re-marriage.

I. SOCIO-ECONOMIC STATUS OF *DALIT* CASTE WOMEN

Table 5.1 reveals that distribution of *dalit* women according to age group, 33.6 per cent respondents were belonged to age group 30 to 35 years whereas 22.8 per cent respondents in 35 to 40 years age group. 18.4 per cent respondents were belonged to 25 to 30 years age group whereas 13.6 per cent respondents in 20 to 25 years age group. 36.8 per cent re-married women were belonged to 30 to 35 years age group whereas 28.8 per cent re-married in 35 to 40 years age group. Age group is an important factor of re-marriage of *Dalit* caste. As *dalit* women know their difficult and hard life, so they easily accept re-marriage. Re-marriage is socially accepted in *dalit* castes and they do

Age

Table 5.1. Distribution of *dalit* women according to age group

Age group (years)	No. of respondents	No. of re-married respondents
20 – 25	34 (13.6)	13 (10.4)
25 – 30	46 (18.4)	20 (16.0)
30 – 35	84 (33.6)	46 (36.8)
35 – 40	57 (22.8)	36 (28.8)
40 – 45	29 (11.6)	10 (8.0)
Total	250 (100.0)	125 (100.0)
χ^2	10.167*	P < 0.05

(Figures in parentheses indicate percentage of respective values)

not feel themselves ashamed due to re-marriage. So they have positive opinion about re-marriage due to social acceptance in their society and they positively accept it also. The observed value of χ^2 (10.167*) was significant at 5.0 per cent level of significance hence, re-marriage was found associated with age.

Education

Table 5.2 shows that distribution of *dalit* women according to education, 54.4 per cent *dalit* women have no education whereas 20.4 per cent women were educated up to primary level. 17.2 per cent women have educated up to middle level, whereas 5.6 per cent women have educated up to high school. 36.8 per cent re-married women have no education whereas 24.0 per cent women have educated up to middle level. Re-married d*alit* women get economical support social security, psychological and emotional support by their husband and family. 90.0 per cent women have educated up to middle level. *Dalit* women has most horrible position in Indian society even today, though the rigidity of untouchability had been

46   Advantages of Re-marriage in Dalit Castes

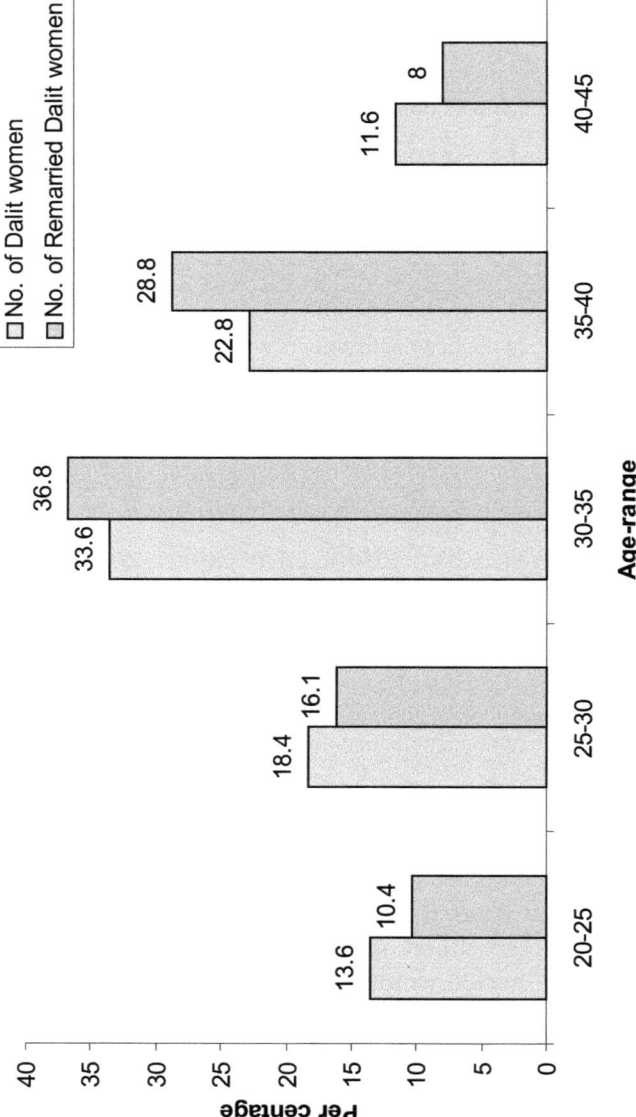

Fig. 5.1. Distribution of *Dalit* Women according to Age group

Findings and Discussion

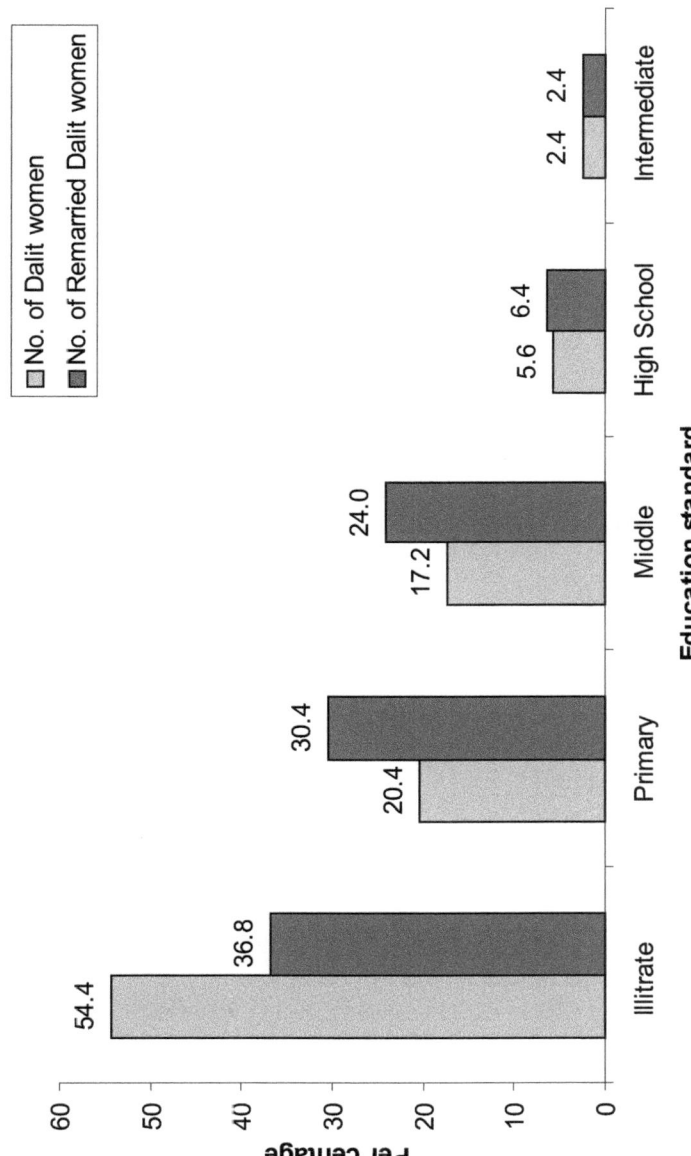

Fig. 5.2. Distribution of *Dalit* Women according to education

relaxed to many extent but status remained almost same.

The observed value of χ^2 (33.497**) was significant at 1.0 per cent level of significance hence re-marriage was also found to be associated with education of the respondents.

Table 5.2. Distribution of *dalit* women according to education

Age group (years)	No. of respondents	No. of re-married respondents
Illiterate	136 (54.4)	46 (36.8)
Primary	51 (20.4)	38 (30.4)
Middle	43 (17.2)	30 (24.0)
High School	14 (5.6)	8 (6.4)
Intermediate	6 (2.4)	3 (2.4)
Total	250 (100.0)	125 (100.0)
χ^2	33.497**	P < 0.01

(Figures in parentheses indicate percentage of respective values)

Type of Family

The perusal of Table 5.3 reveals that distribution of respondents according to type of family, 75.2 per cent *dalit* women were belonged to nuclear family system whereas 24.8 per cent women in joint family system. 88.8 per cent re-married women were belonged to nuclear family while

Table 5.3 Distribution of respondents according to type of family

Type of family	No. of respondents	No. of re-married respondents
Illiterate	136 (54.4)	46 (36.8)
Nuclear	188 (75.2)	111 (88.8)
Joint	62 (24.8)	14 (11.2)
Total	250 (100.0)	125 (100.0)
χ^2	24.794**	P < 0.01

(Figures in parenthesis indicate percentage of respective values)

Findings and Discussion

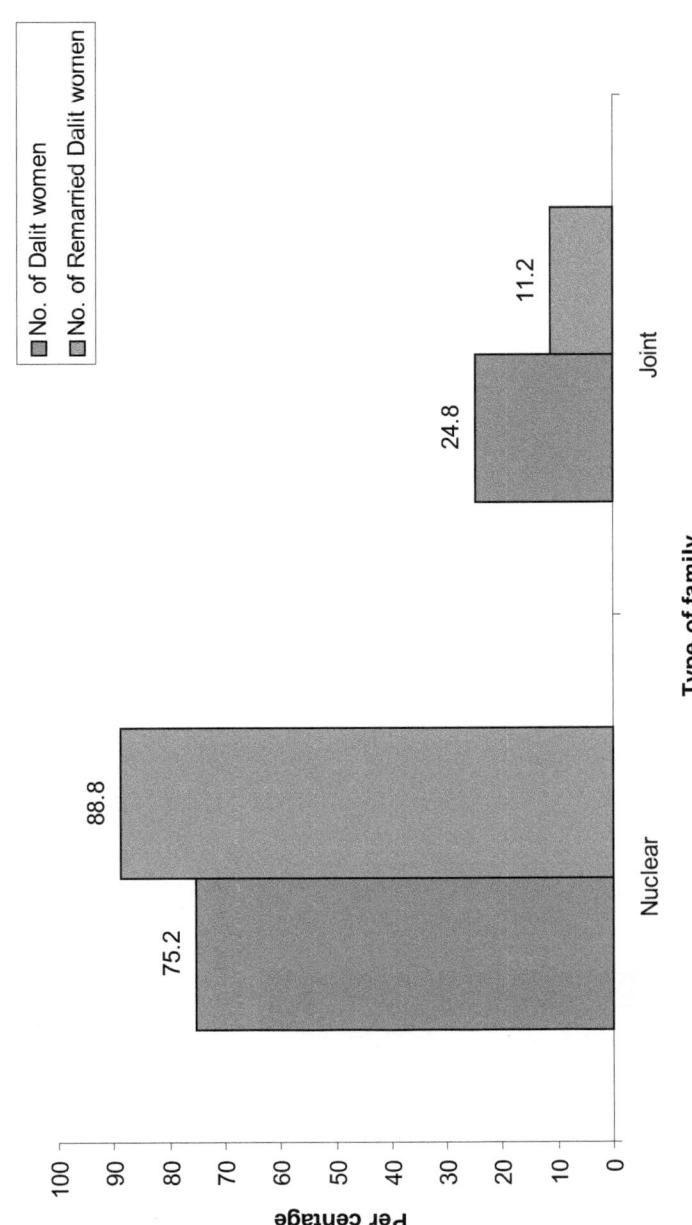

Fig. 5.3. Distribution of *Dalit* Women according to type of family

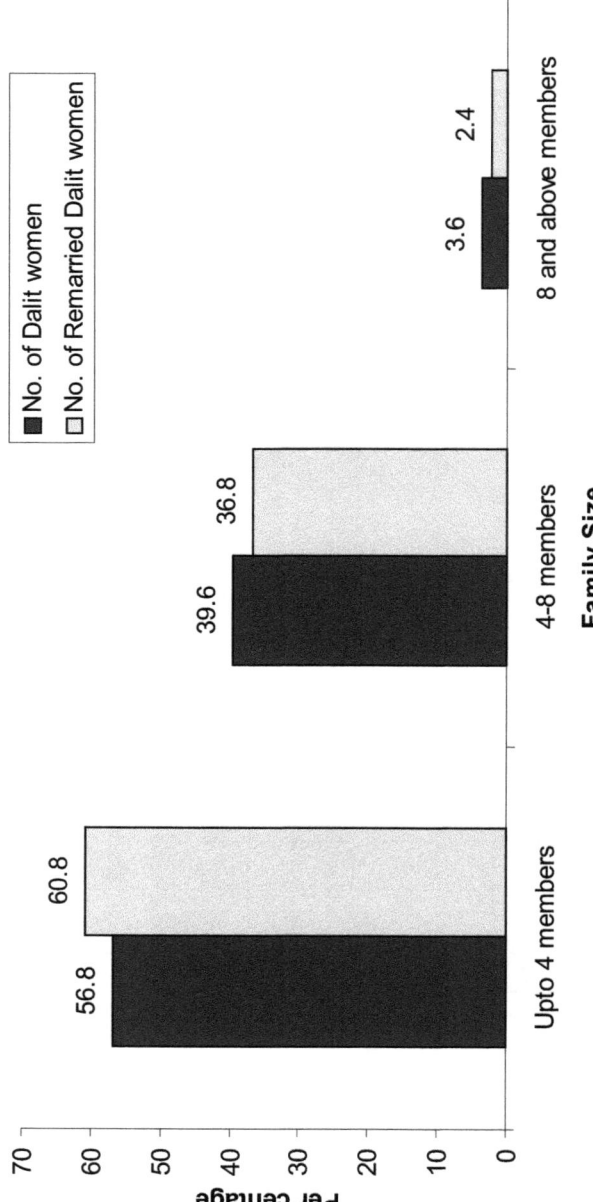

Fig. 5.4. Distribution of *Dalit* Women according to family size

11.2 per cent in joint family. Re-marriage is socially acceptable in *dalit* castes. Even a person having her own children is accepted by re-marriage. Re-marriage give strength to a person because stress of life either, it is due to marital conflicts or any reason is always harmful for a human being. So passing life in isolation or with feeling of burden of life it is better to have a companion as husband for happiness of life. The observed value of χ^2 (24.794**) was significant at 1.0 per cent level of significance hence re-marriage of the respondents was found significantly associated with type of family.

Family Size

Table 5.4 indicates that distribution of respondents according to family size, 56.8 per cent *dalit* women respondents have up to 4 members family size whereas 39.6 per cent respondents have 4 to 8 members family size. 60.8 per cent re-married *dalit* women have up to 4 members family size whereas 36.8 per cent respondents have 4 to 8 members family size. A convincing assessment of the impact of marital instability on the economic status of women therefore requires a credibly exogenous determinant of marital instability. The calculated value of χ^2 is non-significant at 5.0 per cent level of significance.

Table 5.4. Distribution of respondents according to family size

Family size	No. of respondents	No. of re-married respondents
Up to 4 members	142 (56.8)	76 (60.8)
4 to 8 members	9 (39.6)	46 (36.8)
8 & above members	9 (3.6)	3 (2.4)
Total	250 (100.0)	125 (100.0)
χ^2	2.199	P > 0.05

(Figures in parenthesis indicate percentage of respective values)

Type of House

Table 5.5 shows that distribution of respondents according to type of house, 72.0 per cent women have own house while 28.0 per cent respondents have rented house. 65.6 per cent re-married *dalit* women have her own house whereas 34.4 per cent have rented house. As re-marriage is accepted in *dalit* castes due to social economic factors, due to re-marriage *dalit* women get support by their husband social and psychological security by the family. In urban scenario *dalits* are allowed to settle either in a separate colony or in slum areas. The observed value of χ^2 (5.079*) was significant at 5.0 per cent level of significance.

Table 5.5. Distribution of respondents according to type of house

Family size	No. of respondents	No. of re-married respondents
Own	180 (72.0)	82 (65.6)
Rented	70 (28.0)	43 (34.4)
Total	250 (100.0)	125 (100.0)
χ^2	5.079*	P < 0.05

(Figures in parentheses indicate percentage of respective values)

Family Income

Table 5.6. Distribution of respondents according to monthly family income

Family size	No. of respondents	No. of re-married respondents
Up to Rs. 1500	8 (3.2)	-
Rs. 1500 to Rs. 3000	35 (14.0)	12 (9.6)
Rs. 3000 to Rs. 4500	150 (60.0)	88 (70.4)
Rs. 4500 to Rs. 6000	43 (17.2)	21 (16.8)
Rs. 6000 and above	14 (5.6)	4 (3.2)
Total	250 (100.0)	125 (100.0)
χ^2	15.497*	P < 0.05

(Figures in parentheses indicate percentage of respective values)

Findings and Discussion

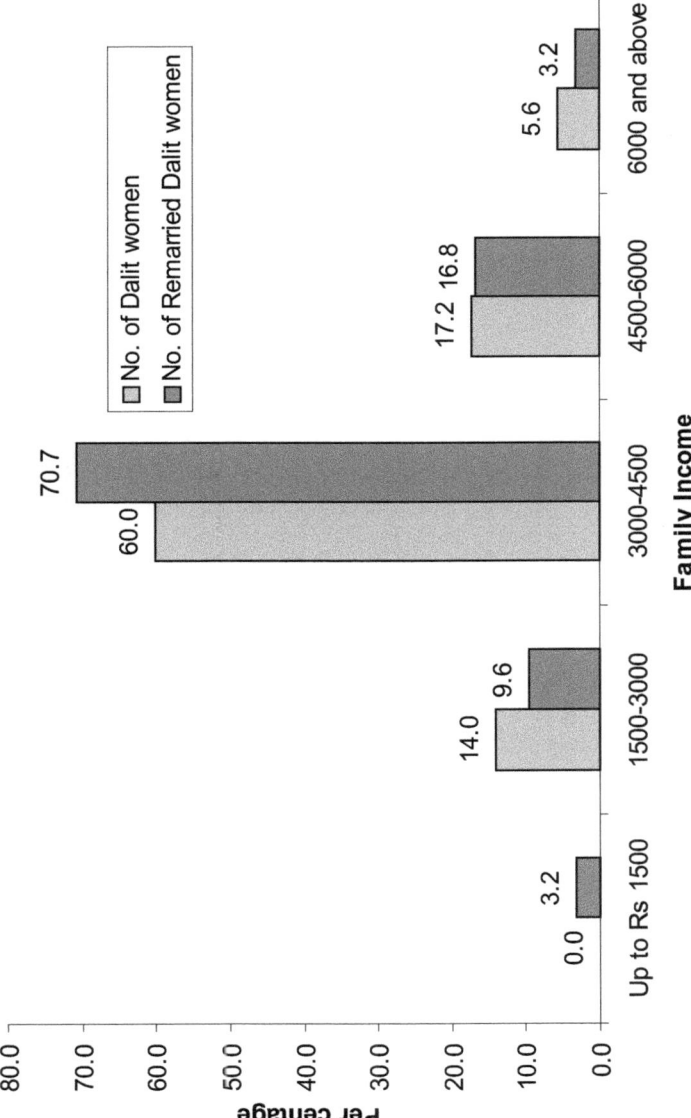

Fig. 5.5. Distribution of Dalit Women according to monthly family Income

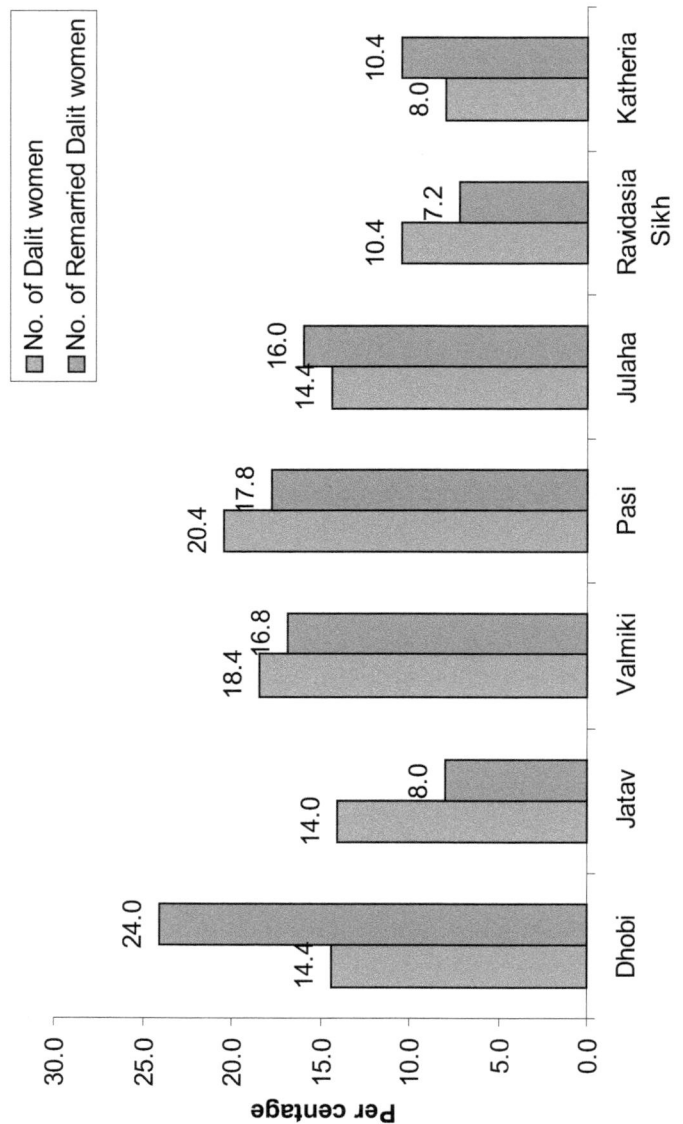

Fig. 5.6. Distribution of Dalit Women according to sub-castes

Table 5.6 reveals that distribution of *dalit* respondents according to monthly family income, 60.0 per cent respondents belonged to Rs. 3000 to Rs. 4500 income group, whereas, 17.2 per cent respondents had earned Rs. 4500 to Rs. 6000 monthly. Only 5.6 per cent respondents were belonged to Rs. 6000 and above income group whereas 3.2 per cent re-married respondents belonged to same income group. 9.6 per cent re-married respondents were belonged to Rs. 1500 to Rs. 3000 monthly income group while 70.4 per cent re-married respondents were belonged to family whose monthly family income Rs. 3,000 to Rs. 4,500. Income is an important factor for re-marriage in *dalit* caste women. As re-marriage is accepted in *dalit* castes due to social economical factors. As *dalit* women has most horrible position in Indian society even today, suffers from molestation etc. This protection may be economical due to re-married *dalit* women get economical support by their husband and she gets rights in husband property also. The observed value of χ^2 (15.497*) was significant at 5.0 per cent level of significance.

Sub Castes

Table 5.7 shows that distribution of *dalit* women respondents according to sub caste, more than 15.0 per cent *dalit* women were belonged to *Valmiki* (18.4) and *Pasi* (26.4) whereas, more than 10.0 per cent women from Dhobi, Jatav (14.0%), Julaha (14.4%) and Ravidasia Sikh (10.4%). In re-married respondents 24.0 per cent women have *Dhobi*, 16.8 per cent *Valmiki*, 17.8 per cent Pasi, 16.0 per cent Julaha and 10.4 per cent Katheria class. Re-marriage is socially acceptable in *dalit* castes. In all sub caste emotional socialization arguments, which claim that males and females respond to stress and manifest distress with different types of emotional problems and marriage is associated with emotional mental health. Depressed women and alcohol abusing men are neither more nor less likely to remain or become married. The observed value of χ^2 (28.443**) was significant at 1.0 per cent level and 6 d.f.

Table 5.7. Distribution of *dalit* women respondents according to sub-castes

Family size	No. of respondents	No. of re-married respondents
Dhobi	36 (14.4)	30 (24.0)
Jatav	35 (14.0)	10 (8.0)
Valmiki	46 (18.4)	21 (16.8)
Pasi	51 (20.4)	22 (17.8)
Julaha	36 (14.4)	20 (16.0)
Ravidasia Sikh	26 (10.4)	9 (7.2)
Katheria	20 (8.0)	13 (10.4)
Total	250 (100.0)	125 (100.0)
χ^2	28.443*	$P < 0.01$

(Figures in parentheses indicate percentage of respective values)

Religion

Table 5.8 reveals that distribution of *dalit* women according to religion, 67.2 per cent *dalit* women have belonged to Hindu family whereas only 14.4 per cent women from Muslim family. 66.4 per cent re-married women have belonged to Hindu family, whereas 16.0 per cent women from Muslim family. Above data shows that 10.4 per cent *dalit*

Table 5.8. Distribution of respondents according to religion

Religion	No. of respondents	No. of re-married respondents
Hindu	168 (67.2)	83 (66.4)
Muslim	36 (14.4)	20 (16.0)
Sikh	26 (10.4)	9 (7.2)
Christian	20 (8.0)	13 (10.4)
Total	250 (100.0)	125 (100.0)
χ^2	4.730	$P > 0.05$

(Figures in parentheses indicate percentage of respective values)

Findings and Discussion 57

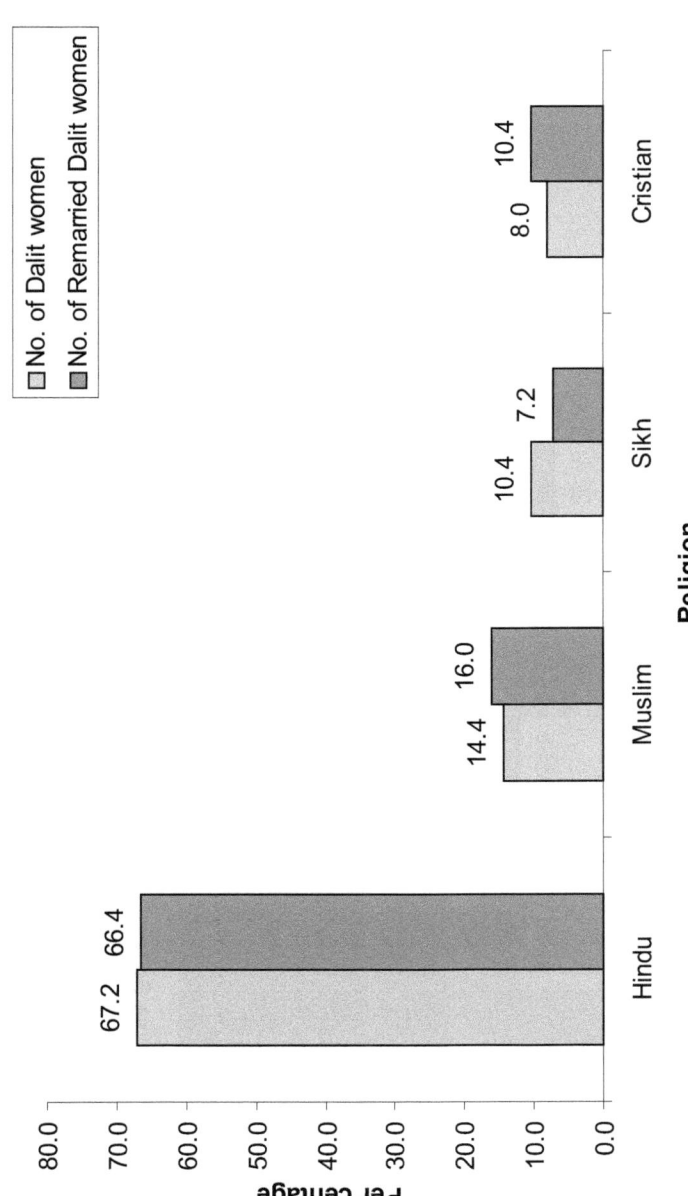

Fig. 5.7. Distribution of Dalit Women according to religion

Advantages of Re-marriage in Dalit Castes

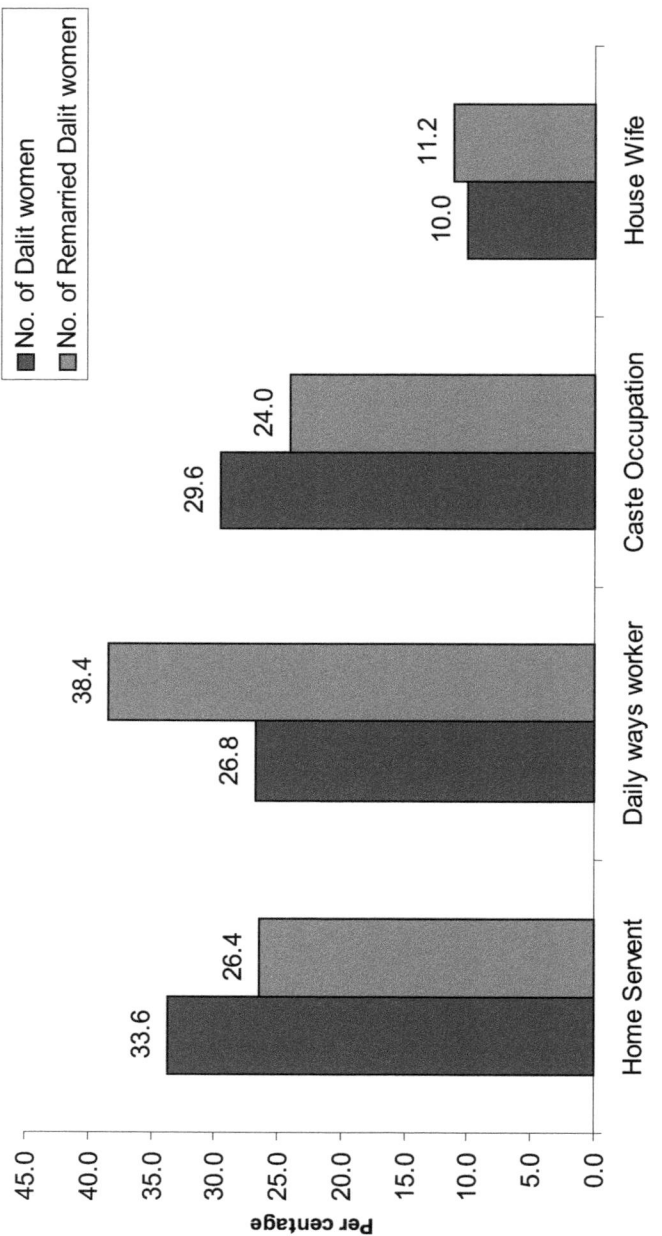

Fig. 5.8. Distribution of Dalit women according to occupation

Findings and Discussion

women have belonged to Sikh religion and 8.0 per cent women from Christian. 7.2 per cent re-married women from Sikh religion whereas 10.4 per cent women from Christian community. All major religions have their own laws which govern divorces within their own community and separate regulations exist regarding divorce in interfaith marriages. The law regarding Hindus allows divorce to be granted on the grounds of infidelity of either husband or wife. The Christian law, however, would traditionally not have granted a divorce to a women solely on the grounds of adultery. She would have had to prove another violation such as cruelty. The three main components of desertion are the "disruption of cohabitation, absence of just or reasonable cause and their combination throughout three years.

Occupation

The perusal of Table 5.9 reveals that distribution of *dalit* women according to occupation, 33.6 per cent *dalit* women engaged in jobs like home servant and 29.6 per cent women in caste occupation. 26.8 per cent *dalit* women have daily wages worker while 38.4 per cent re-married women respondents were engaged in same occupation. 26.4 per cent re-married women were home servant only. 11.2 per cent respondents were house wife. The contribution of scheduled

Table 5.9. Distribution of *dalit* women according to occupation

Religion	No. of respondents	No. of re-married respondents
Home servant	84 (33.6)	33 (26.4)
Daily wages worker	67 (26.8)	48 (38.4)
Caste occupation	74 (29.6)	30 (24.0)
House wife	25 (10.0)	14 (11.2)
Total	250 (100.0)	125 (100.0)
χ^2	44.058**	$P < 0.01$

(Figures in parenthesis indicate percentage of respective values)

castes women to the economic development in country is significant especially in daily wages worker and caste occupation. The scheduled castes are largely concentrated in labour and sweepers and condition is very deplorable their working condition is poor and the remuneration is also very poor. The observed value of χ^2 (44.058**) was significant at 1.0 per cent level of significance hence re-marriage of women dependented their occupation.

Table 5.10. Distribution of women respondents as per husband occupation

Husband occupation	Frequency	Per cent
Vegetable seller	16	6.4
Rickshaw driver	9	3.6
Chat seller	11	4.4
Cloth seller	24	9.6
Security guard	26	10.4
Daily wages worker	115	46.0
Sweeper	28	11.2
Caste occupation	21	8.4
Total	250	100.0

It is evident from Table 5.10 that distribution of women respondents as per husband occupation, 46.0 per cent women's husband were daily wages worker whereas 6.4 per cent vegetable seller, 3.6 per cent rickshaw driver, 4.4 per cent chat seller and 9.6 per cent cloth seller, all they were doing hard work in whole day. 8.4 per cent women's husband were engaged in caste occupation, according his caste like shoes melding, washing cloths and their cutting. In the male dominated society, polygamy is allowed and more so in many *dalits* families, the condition of scavenger and sweeper is very deplorable and they the most vulnerable sectors among scheduled castes. The working condition is very poor and the remuneration is also very poor.

Findings and Discussion

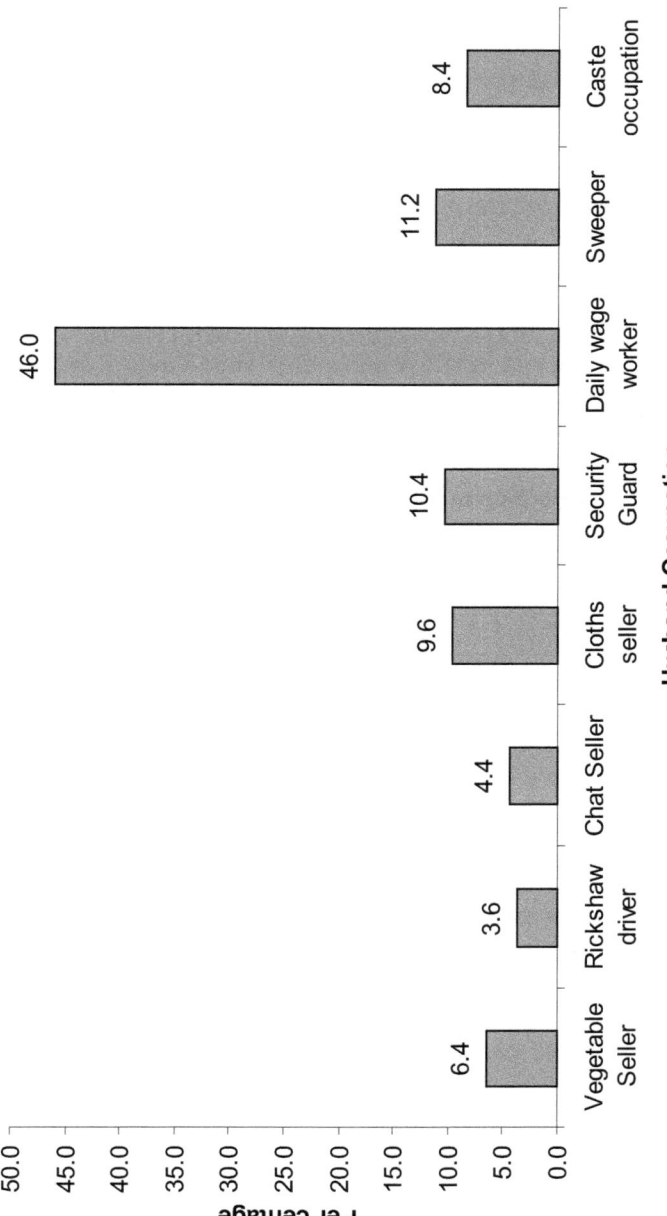

Fig. 5.9. Distribution of Dalit Women according to husband occupation

Marital Status

Table 5.11 reveals that distribution of *dalit* women according to marital status, 50.0 per cent *dalit* women under study area were re-married whereas 36.8 per cent women married. 7.2 per cent women in study area were divorce and 6.0 per cent women were widow. As re-marriage is accepted in *dalit* castes due to social economical factors. Re-marriage give emotional support and protect the life of woman also. Marital loss has harmful, while gain has beneficial, consequences for men's and women's mental health. In so far as males and females respond to stress with sex typical emotional problems, regardless of marital status, women have more depressed than men. But there are no gender differences in the association between marital status and depression, benefits of marriage for depression apply equally to women and men.

Table 5.11. Distribution of *dalit* women according to marital status

Marital status	Frequency	Per cent
Married	92	36.8
Divorcee	18	7.2
Re-married	125	50.0
Widow	15	6.0
Total	250	100.0

Economic Status

Table 5.12 and Fig. 5.11 reveal that 59.2 per cent *dalit* women were earner whereas 32.0 per cent women were helper. 56.8 per cent re-married women were as a earner whereas 8.0 per cent women were dependent like housewife. *Dalit* women had to go for wage earning due to high rate of poverty. As wage earner obviously they had better respect since family had to depend at least partly on their income. In respect of *dalit* craftsman like the *Jatav*, women participate in production activity and thus part of economic chain. In respect of some caste like Hadi, women help in delivering child in respect of all caste and thus were

Findings and Discussion

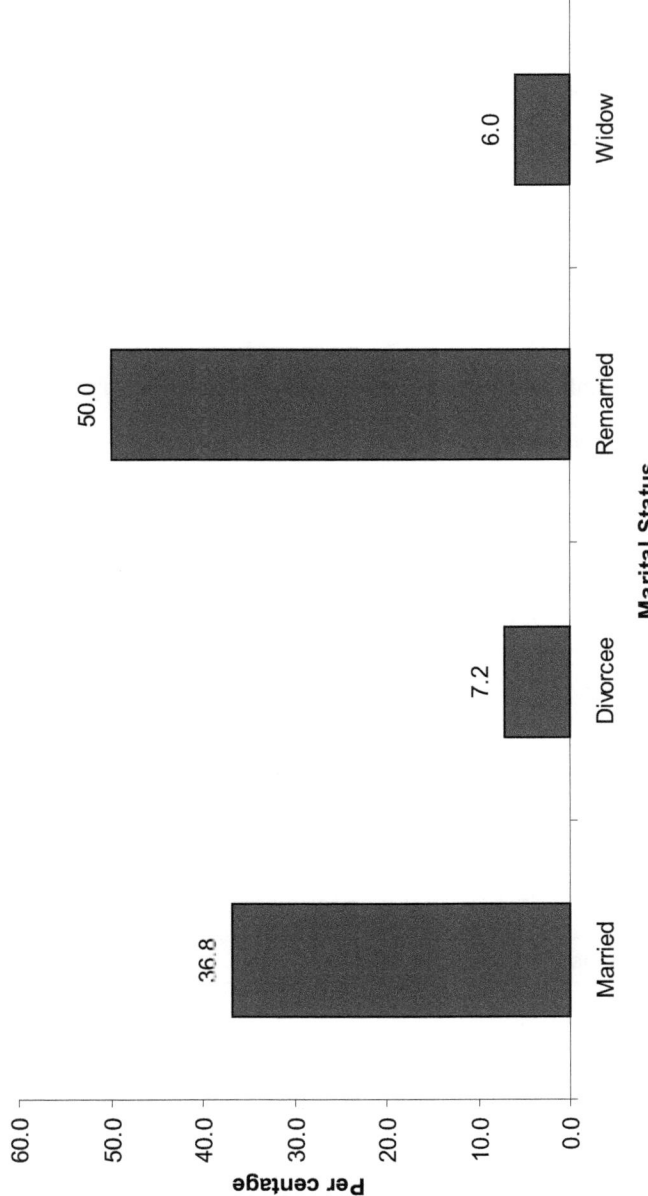

Fig. 5.10. Distribution of Dalit Women according to marital status

considered often like lady doctors. The observed value of χ^2 was non-significant at 5.0 per cent level of significance.

Table 5.12. Distribution of respondents according to economic status

Religion	No. of respondents	No. of re-married respondents
Earner	148 (59.2)	71 (56.8)
Helper	80 (32.0)	44 (35.2)
Dependent	22 (8.8)	10 (8.0)
Total	250 (100.0)	125 (100.0)
χ^2	1.225	P > 0.05

(Figures in parentheses indicate percentage of respective values)

Material Possession

Table 5.13 reveals that distribution of respondents according to material possession, more than 90 per cent *dalit* women have possessed cooking gas and seiling fan while in

Table 5.13. Distribution of *dalit* women respondents according to material possession

Items	Frequency of respondents	Frequency of re-married respondents
Cooking gas	228 (91.2)	69 (55.2)
Double bed	8 (3.2)	3 (2.4)
Sofa set	15 (6.0)	11 (8.8)
Television	202 (80.8)	119 (95.2)
DVD player	31 (12.4)	18 (14.4)
Sewing machine	36 (14.4)	21 (16.8)
Steel almirah	30 (12.0)	22 (17.6)
Seiling fan	230 (92.0)	122 (97.6)
Refrigerator	39 (15.6)	24 (19.2)
Motor cycle	28 (11.2)	17 (13.6)

(Figures in parentheses indicate percentage of respective values)

Findings and Discussion

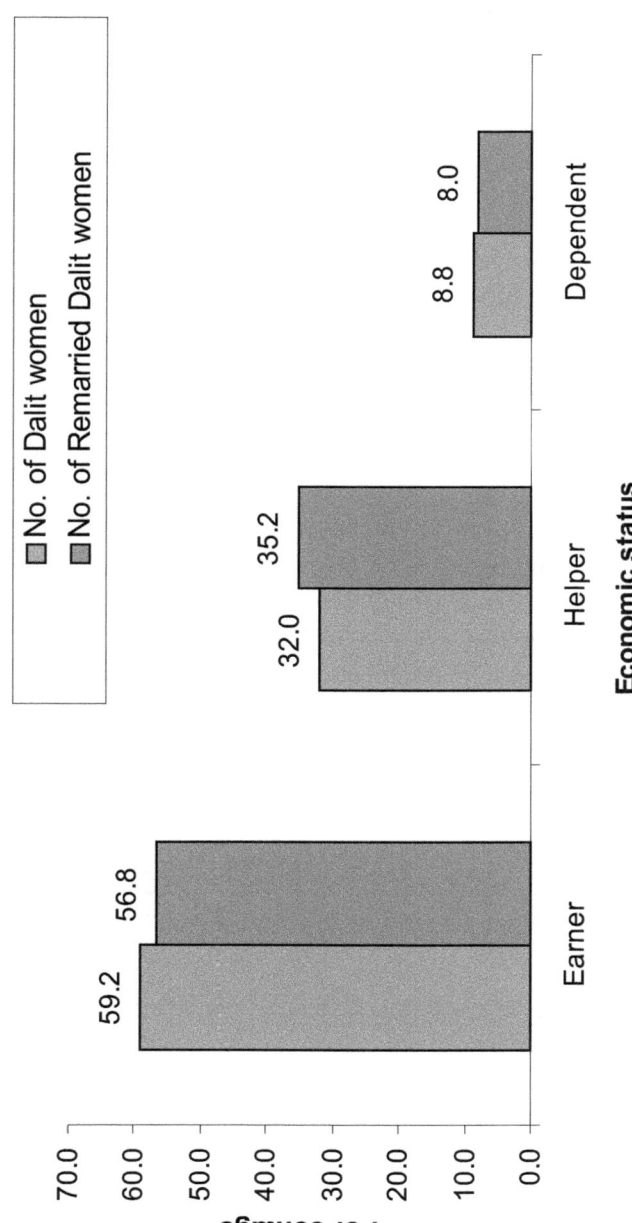

Fig. 5.11. Distribution of Dalit Women according to economic status

re-married respondents have cooking gas, television and seiling fan. Less than 15.0 per cent respondents of the study area have double bed, sofa set, DVD player (12.4%), steel almirah (12.0%) and motor cycle (11.2%) whereas in re-married *dalit* women have double bed (2.4%), sofa set (8.8%) and motor cycle (13.6%). The economic condition of the *dalit* women also reveals the low position that they occupied in the hierarchy of the society. Mostly they worked as landless labourers and as domestic servants, their working condition is very poor.

II. VIEWS OF THE RESPONDENTS REGARDING RE-MARRIAGE

Table 5.14 directed that views regarding re-marriage of *dalit* women, 52.8 per cent women have given views for reason of harassment whereas 42.4 per cent women have showed dissatisfaction from physical relations. 40.8 per cent women were given views about economical problem whereas 39.2 per cent women shows extra marital relationships.

Table 5.14. Views of respondents regarding re-marriage

Views	Yes	No	Scores
Death of first husband	43 (34.4)	82 (65.6)	0.34
Reason of harassment	66 (52.8)	59 (47.2)	0.53
Marriage conflicts	31 (24.8)	94 (75.2)	0.25
Unsatisfaction from physical relations	53 (42.4)	72 (57.6)	0.42
Economical problem	51 (40.8)	74 (59.2)	0.41
Extra marital relationship	49 (39.2)	76 (60.8)	0.39
H.I.V. positive	8 (6.4)	117 (93.6)	0.06
Domestic violence	43 (34.4)	82 (65.6)	0.34
Giving birth too much girls	26 (20.8)	99 (79.2)	0.21

(Figures in parentheses indicate percentage of respective values)

Several concerns motivate the importance of identifying the causal relationship between divorce and the economic status of women. Information will contribute to a better understanding of the underlying causes of gender inequality in the India. Divorced women might possibly improve their economic position by cohabitating or remarrying. Maximum score given by respondents are harassment, main reasons for remarring. Economic independence would accelerate the improvement of the status of women. Government would endeavour to give joint titles to husband and wife in all development activities involving house-sites and beneficiary oriented economic units. The economic emancipation of the family with specific attention to women, education of children and family planning will constitute the three major operational aspects of the family centered poverty alleviation strategy. SC/ST girl's remains uneducated, they got married very early. Marriage in the high reproductive stage with high fertility rate, children care more, the burden fell on the young girls which affected their health. They were not able to assist in family matters to their husbands. The contribution of scheduled castes women to the economic development of country is significant especially in the agricultural sector. The condition of scavenger and sweeper is very deplorable and they are most vulnerable sectors among scheduled castes. Male dominated society, polygamy is a allowed and more so in many *dalit* families and in this position of the women deteriorated. Rural women were more blessed than urban women because divorce and re-marriage were allowed for them. Mainly low caste family allowed divorce and re-marriage for their women maximum score given by re-married respondents by early age at first marriage followed by economic factors.

Promoting Factors for Re-marriage of *Dalit* Castes

(a) Social Factors : Despite advances in standard of living of the population, the condition of widows and divorced

women remains deplorable in society. The situation is worse in developing nations with their unique social, cultural and economic milieu, which at times ignores the basic human rights of this vulnerable section of society. A gap exists in life expectancies of men and women in both developing and developed nations. This, coupled with greater re-marriage rates in men, ensures that the number of widows continues to exceed that of widowers.

A. Social Factors

Table 5.15 shows that social factors for re-marriage of *dalit* women, 57.6 per cent women in early age at marriage while 36.8 per cent women re-married due to economic predictors and non-marital sex respectively. 30.4 per cent re-married women have faced religion factors whereas 48.8 per cent women were faced parental marriage in early aged. Re-marriage provides social support, increase the level of health and well being and improves financial standing. It is said that the death of a spouse causes the economic and

Table 5.15. Promoting factors for re-marriage of *dalit* caste

Social factors	Always	Some-times	Never	Sco-res
Parental marriage	61 (48.8)	28 (22.4)	36 (28.8)	1.20
Early age at first marriage	72 (57.6)	39 (31.2)	14 (11.2)	1.46
Homogamy	12 (9.6)	25 (20.0)	88 (70.4)	0.39
Educational attainment	43 (34.4)	66 (52.8)	16 (12.8)	1.22
Religion	38 (30.4)	31 (24.8)	56 (44.8)	0.86
Economic predictors	46 (36.8)	72 (57.6)	7 (5.6)	1.31
Non-marital sex	46 (36.8)	48 (38.4)	31 (24.8)	1.12
Cohabitation	24 (19.2)	37 (29.6)	64 (51.2)	0.68

(Figures in parentheses indicate percentage of respective values)

physical health of the surviving spouse to decline. Re-marriage is one way to reduce this decline. Ex-husband might have always been the one making the money while she took care of the house and children. Another reason women might not want to remarry is future reproduction but intentionality positiveness, depth and honesty of disclosure was positively associated with.

B. Cultural Factors

Table 5.16 reveals that cultural factors for re-marriage of *dalit* women, 59.2 per cent re-married women were faced risk of hyper individualism whereas 44.8 per cent women deinstitutionalization of marriage. Only 21.6 per cent women always faced fragility of soulmate marriage whereas 42.4 per cent women faced sometimes soulmate marriage. *Dalit* is term for a group of people traditionally regarded as untouchables or of low caste. Gandhi's coinage of the word Harijon, translated roughly as "children of God". There are about 250 million *dalits* in India. There is meager improvement in the socio-economic condition of *dalits* in the past 50 years. *Dalit* women faced the triple burden of caste, class and gender. Most of *dalits* women continue to live in extreme poverty, without land or opportunities for better employment or education.

Table 5.16. Promoting factors for re-marriage of *dalit* caste

Social factors	Always	Some-times	Never	Sco-res
Deinstitionalization of marriage	56 (44.8)	31 (24.8)	38 (30.4)	1.14
Fragility of soulmate marriage	27 (21.6)	53 (42.4)	45 (36.0)	0.86
Risk of hyper individualism	74 (59.2)	33 (26.4)	18 (14.4)	1.45

(Figures in parentheses indicate percentage of respective values)

C. Religious Factors

Table 5.17 indicates that religious factors for re-marriage of *dalit* women, 73.6 per cent women were faced in Muslim community whereas 70.4 per cent women in Christian religion. Muslim society in India can also be separated into several caste like groups in contradiction to the teachings Islam, descendents of indigenous lower caste converts are discriminated against by "noble" or "ashraf". The *dalit* Muslims are referred to by the Ashraf and Ajlaf Muslims are Arzal. Ambedkar wrote about the *dalit* Muslims and was extremely critical of their mistreatment by upper caste Muslims "within these groups there are castes with social precedence of exactly the same nature as one finds among the Hindus". *Dalit* Christian faced economic and social hardships due to discrimination by upper caste priests and nuns. Most *dalits* continue to live in extreme poverty without land or opportunities for better employment or education. The *dalit* Christians are still carrying the cross of humiliation, exploitation, oppression and sub-jugation. *Dalit* women are also raped as a form of retaliation. Women of scheduled castes and scheduled tribes are raped as part of an effort by upper caste leaders to support movements to demand payment to minimum wages. 20.8 per cent women were faced religious factors due to Sikh whereas 55.2 per cent women were faced factors due to Hinduism. *Dalits* form a class among the Sikhs who stratify their society according to traditional casteism Kanshi Ram himself was of Sikh background although

Table 5.17. Promoting factors for re-marriage of *dalit* caste

Religious factors	Yes	No	Scores
Hindu	69 (55.2)	56 (44.8)	0.55
Muslim	92 (73.6)	33 (26.4)	0.74
Sikh	26 (20.8)	99 (79.2)	0.21
Christian	88 (70.4)	37 (29.6)	0.70

(Figures in parenthesis indicate percentage of respective values)

Findings and Discussion

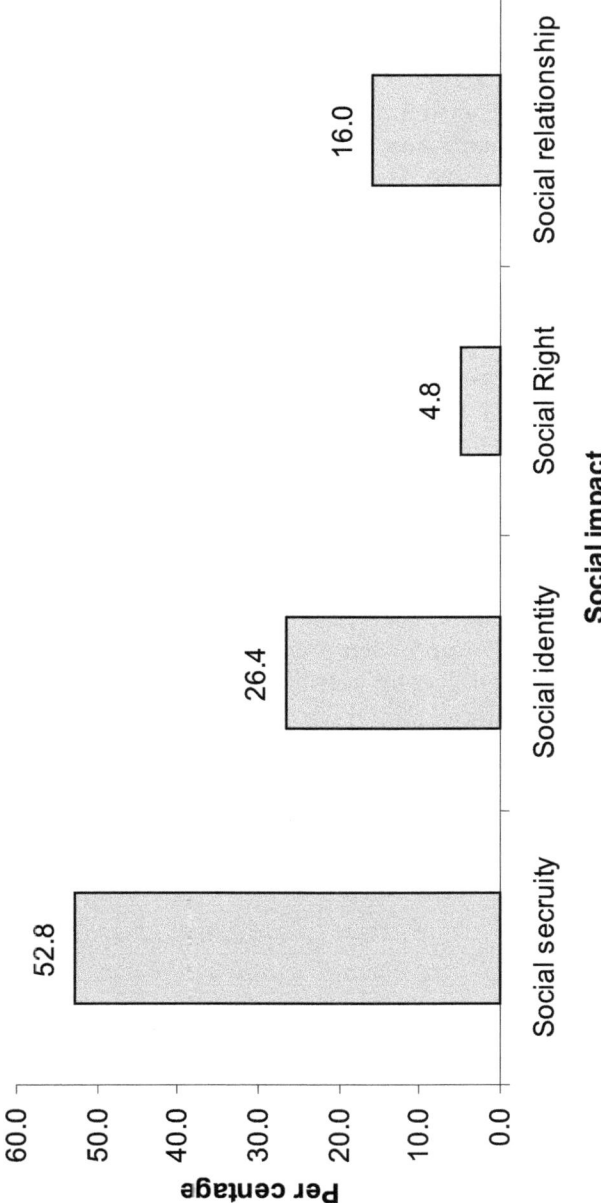

Fig. 5.12. Social impact of re-marriage on Dalit Castes

converted because he found the Sikh society did not respect *dalits* and so became a new-Buddhist. The different Sikh *dalits* are Ravidasa Sikh and Mazhabi Sikh Although Sikhism does not recognize the caste system, many families, especially the ones with immediate cultural ties to India generally do not marry among different castes, other Sikh groups include Jhiwars, Bazigars, Rai Sikh just as with Hindu *dalits*, there has been violence against Sikh *dalits*. Hindu *dalit* women mostly *chamar*, *pasi* and *dhobi* were continue to live in extreme poverty, without land or opportunities for better employment or education. *Dalit* women faced the triple burden of caste, class and gender. There is meager improvement in the socio-economic condition of *dalits* in the past 50 years. More religious factors were involved in Muslim community in reference to re-marriage.

D. Other Factors

Table 5.18 indicates that promoting factors for re-marriage, 63.2 per cent *dalit* women have faced lack of money whereas 42.4 per cent women have faced employment. 54.4 per cent women were faced empowerment whereas 18.4 per cent women were faced lower educational status for re-marriage. 8.8 per cent women have always affected by serials

Table 5.18. Promoting factors for re-marriage of *dalit* caste

Social factors	Always	Sometimes	Never	Scores
Lack of money	79 (63.2)	38 (30.4)	8 (6.4)	1.57
Employment	53 (42.4)	40 (32.0)	32 (25.6)	1.17
Empowerment	68 (54.4)	43 (34.4)	14 (11.2)	1.43
Educational status	23 (18.4)	38 (30.4)	64 (51.2)	0.67
Strong economic background	17 (13.6)	43 (34.4)	65 (52.0)	0.62
Serials	11 (8.8)	55 (44.0)	59 (47.2)	0.62

(Figures in parentheses indicate percentage of respective values)

and other shows. Fear of alienation of women from their environment as a result of education for low literacy level among scheduled castes women. In some areas there are complaints from *dalit* women teachers of misbehaviours, blackmail and exploitation by the male staff of other high caste people. The girls were forced to do domestic chores which prevent them from attending school and working to earn for the family prevent the girls from attending school. *Dalit* girls working with parents to earn their livelihood in beedi factories or other unorganized sector made them illiterate. Social restriction is that the women should stop education after marriage.

Re-marriage fulfils needs for love and companionship, instrumental benefits of re-marriage may also be high. Poverty rates are typically the lowest in married couple households, and thus re-marriage after divorce may represent an important route out of poverty for women and their children. More broadly, it examines the relative effects of men's and women's socio-economic prospects on the propensity to remarry. The conclusion of most research analyzing the economic consequences of divorce is that the economic status of women deteriorates following divorce, while men's financial position improves. Men are expected to see an immediate improvement in their economic situation following divorce or separation because personal income generally remains stable while the number of dependents is reduced. It is also well established that few men pay large amounts in alimony and child support following divorce or separation.

Because of the relatively greater importance of economic pressures for women to remarry, resources may have a greater effect on women's than men's propensity to remarry. Past research investigates how men's resources affect their propensity to remarry, although the impact of resources held by women is relatively neglected. Women's increasing economic independence during this period is a common explanation for the decline in first marriage rates. Women's rising income is translated into reduced economic dependence on a spouse, causing women to feel less economic incentive to marry. The economic independence argument is theoretically grounded in Gary Becker's (1981) "gains to trade" model of marriage. Becker views men and women as trading partners, and believes marriage occurs only if the perceived gains to marriage are positive, and if both partners believe they will be better off married than single.

III. IMPACT OF SOCIOLOGICAL, ECONOMIC AND PSYCHOLOGICAL STATUS OF *DALIT* WOMEN REGARDING RE-MARRIAGE

Table 5.19 reveals that social impact of re-marriage of *dalit* women, 52.8 per cent women have social security for re-married whereas, 26.4 per cent women have social identity for re-married. 16.0 per cent women were increase social relationship whereas 4.8 per cent re-married women were wants social right. In most cases re-marriage will not have any impact on child support. The new husband is not legally responsible for the children. The father may have a tight budget and paying child support is a financial hardship. Meanwhile, the ex-wife and children are living an affluent life. The situation changes dramatically if the mother's new husband adopts the minor children. In this scenario the step father becomes a legal father to the children and is no longer responsible for ongoing support of the children. Every *dalit*

Table 5.19. Social impact of re-marriage of *dalit* caste

Economical impact	Frequency	Per cent
Social security	66	52.8
Social identity	33	26.4
Social right	6	4.8
Increase social relationship	20	16.0
Total	125	100.0

women have their own ideas and hopes about their futures, but sometimes life takes a wrong turn, and for some this means divorce or the death of a spouse.

Table 5.20. Economic impact of re-marriage of *dalit* caste

Economical impact	Frequency	Per cent
Economical security	78	62.4
Spend luxuries life	14	11.2
Remove pressure of self earning	33	26.4
Total	125	100.0

Table 5.20 reveals that economic impact of re-marriage of *dalit* women, 62.4 per cent women have re-married due to economical security whereas 26.4 per cent women were re-married for remove pressure of self-earning. A divorce case does not necessarily end when the one party is ordered to pay maintenance, also known as alimony to the other party, remarrying will not have any impact on child support. The new husband is not legally responsible for the children. The children are the responsibility of their parents. Because the children are well taken care of by the mother and step father. The father feels his support is not necessary, at least not at the level he has been playing. The child remain the responsibility of their parents. The court can't force the step father to provide for the children and will not take his income into account. In extremely rare cases a court might grant the father a reduction from his child support if the parties financial conditions suggest it is in the best interest of the children. The burden for this type of adjustment is very high and the reduction will not usually be granted. The situation changes dramatically if the mother's new husband adopts the minor children, in this scenario the step father becomes a legal father of the children and is now required to provide for them. The natural father is no longer responsible for ongoing support of the children.

Advantages of Re-marriage in Dalit Castes

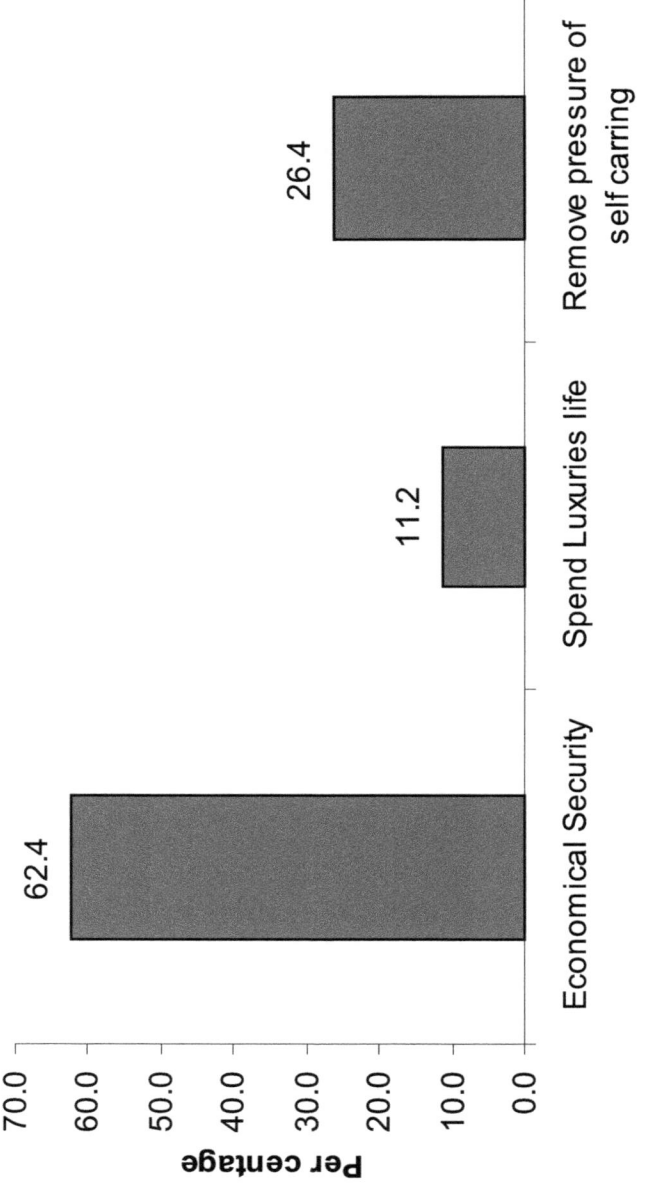

Fig. 5.13. Economical impact of remarriage on dalit castes

Findings and Discussion

Table 5.21. Psychological impact of re-marriage of *dalit* caste

Economical impact	Frequency	Per cent
To feel secure	46	36.8
Relief from mental stress	22	17.6
Develop decision making ability	3	2.4
Minimize life stress	11	8.8
Social support	13	10.4
Physical security	30	24.0
Total	125	100.0

Table 5.21 shows that psychological impact of re-married women respondents, 36.8 per cent women have to feel secure whereas 24.0 per cent have faced physical security. 17.6 per cent women respondents have relief from mental stress whereas 8.8 per cent women respondents have herself minimize life stress due to re-married. Re-marriage is one way to reduce this decline in late life might occur when the spouse is a widow or widower whose first marriage was viewed as successful, therefore, continuing their habitual disclosure patterns, but to a lesser depth in the re-marriage. A spouse who has been will fully and definitively abandoned by his or her partner, who refuses to be reconciled and is unwilling to fulfill the obligations of the marriage covenant despite persistent persuasion may seek a legal divorce, which in such a case constitutes a public recognition of a marriage already broken and remarry.

Re-marriage provides social support, increases the level of health and well-being, and improves financial standing. This study also tries to determine whether being married make people happier. Reasons to support this claim are companionship, support, assistance for those with disability, and available sexual activity that provides satisfaction and aerobic exercise. This study found that those who have not re-married for a long time, or those who are living with

Fig. 5.14. Psychological Impact of re-marriage on Dalit Castes

another person are less likely to remarry, while those who are well educated and in good health are more likely to remarry.

I know in may own personal life I few elderly women who lost their husbands due to illness, and neither of the women re-married. Both ladies were healthy, and lived by themselves after the death of their spouses. I don't think either would have been any happier if they had re-married. They seemed very content, perhaps because they had family members and friends to support them, and were active in the community. Moreover, with women becoming more educated, economically independent and aware of their rights, divorce rates are increasing along with associated psychological ramifications. The fact that widowed/divorced women suffer from varying psychological stressors is often ignored. It has been concluded in various studies that such stressors could be harbingers of psychiatric illnesses (e.g. depression, anxiety, substance dependence), and hence should be taken into account by treating physicians, society is required before these women get their rightful place, for which a strong will is needed in the minds of the people, and in law-governing bodies.

As directed from table 5.22 shows that social barriers of other caste women in re-marriage, 53.2 per cent women faced physical illness whereas 64.8 per cent other caste women were faced disagreement of children so they were not prepared herself for re-marriage. 38.4 per cent women were faced disagreement of family or parents whereas 32.4 per cent women have faced caste problems. Other caste women just like subordinate in family for every decision, she waits for the man's opinion (he might be father, brother, husband or a son) and there is paternal domination even though a women may be an earning member, to earn for the family is another essential duty. Moreover, she has to give money to her alcoholic husband to satisfy his addiction. She has to do all the domestic work and male members in the family do not help her for they think it is degrading for the male to do

Table 5.22. Social barriers in re-marriage of other castes women

Barriers	Yes	No	Scores	Rank
Disagreement of family	96 (38.4)	154 (61.6)	1.38	III
Caste problems	81 (32.4)	169 (67.6)	1.32	IV
Disagreement of children	162 (64.8)	88 (35.2)	1.65	I
Physical illness	133 (53.2)	117 (46.8)	1.53	II
Lack of education	61 (24.4)	189 (75.6)	1.24	V
Social acceptability	32 (12.8)	218 (87.2)	1.13	VI
Lack of independent	28 (11.2)	222 (88.8)	1.13	VII

(Figures in parenthesis indicate percentage of respective values)

such work. In illiterate other caste families a women is always treated with such low esteem that she has a status of nothing more than a more slipper worn by the men and she also regards herself as inferior to a men. She has to tolerate suspicion about her character and wicked mental torture yet she has the freedom to remarry. A other caste women is financially deprived, being uneducated the other caste women in general have the least sense about health and general hygiene. 12.8 per cent other caste women were faced social barrier about social acceptability and 11.2 per cent other caste women have faced social barriers due to lack of independency in her life.

Table 5.23. Correlation coefficient between independent variables and various factors of *dalit* women respondents

Variables	Sociological	Economic	Psychological
Age	0.2613	0.2647	0.3319
Education	0.1973	0.3160	−0.2203
Family size	0.0211	+0.3751	0.2981
Income	0.3370	−0.2116	−0.2913
Marital status	−0.1097	−0.3617	+0.1094
Occupation	0.3045	−0.3553	0.3161

Findings and Discussion

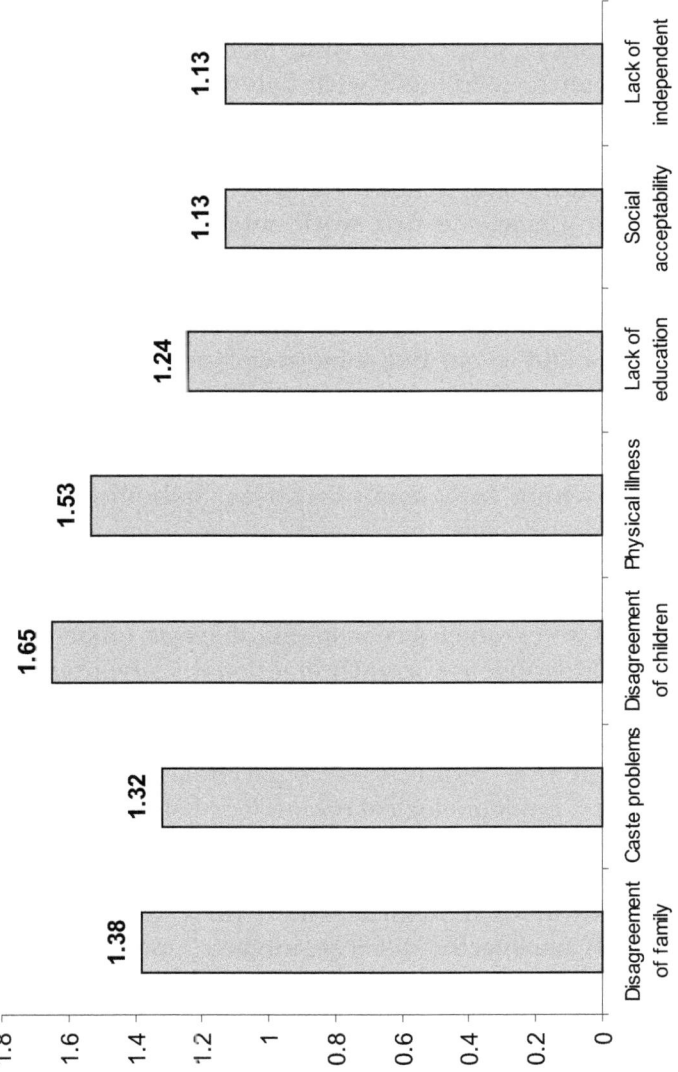

Fig. 5.15. Social Barriers in re-marriage of other castes women

Table 5.23 reveals that correlation coefficient between independent variables and factors like sociological, economic and psychological of *dalit* women, sociological factor of *dalit* women positively correlated with their age, income, education and occupation (0.3045*). Economic factors of *dalit* women was significantly correlated with age (0.2647), education (0.3160*) and family size (0.3751*). Psychological factors of respondents was significantly correlated with their age (0.3319*), family size (0.2981*) and occupation (0.3161*). Women who manage to find work outside home not only have to leave their children unsupervised but also find their income too meager for the family. Out of such situations arise problems of child labour, juvenile delinquency, disorganized personalities and so on. But some sociological factors have been undertaken to analyze this problems of desertion. Divorce, however, has come in the last few decades. All marriages cannot succeed, some end in disharmony, in some marriages which fail, some fatalists, believing in an inescapable destiny, just drag on and pull over, some optimists who think that happiness is a state of mind try to readjust themselves, but some break their marriages. Psychological symptoms of women such as nonspecific distress, anxiety and depression. Marriage is currently emotionally advantageous for men and disadvantageous for women, as well as question the wisdom of focusing exclusively on social roles for explaining gender differences in psychological distress among adults. Epidemiological research on both lifetime and recent prevalence rates of mental disorders consistently demonstrates that while women have higher rates of affective and anxiety disorders and their psychological corollaries of nonspecific distress, anxiety and depression. Females manifest distress with different types of emotional problems role arguments are most useful for explaining differences in mental health among women. Marital loss has harmful while marital gain has beneficial consequences for women's mental health.

Table 5.24 shows that correlation coefficient between independent variables and factors of re-married *dalit* women, sociological factors of *dalit* re-married women were positively correlated with their age (0.4133*), education (0.4161*) and occupation. Economic factors of re-married women was positively correlated with age (0.5132*) and family size. Psychological factors of re-married *dalit* women was positive and significantly correlated with age (0.5538*), family size and occupation (0.4320*). According to education, income and occupation of the respondent were increase than decrease the economic factors and psychological factors were also decreased. Marital status differences in socio-demographic characteristics such as age, education,

Table 5.24. Correlation coefficient between independent variables and various factors of re-married *dalit* women

Variables	Sociological	Economic	Psychological
Age	0.4133*	0.5132*	0.5538*
Education	0.4161*	−0.2819	−0.4612
Family size	−0.2180	0.5712*	0.5973*
Income	0.1854	−0.3540	−0.5261
Occupation	0.4453*	−0.2661	0.4320*

(*significant at 5.0%)

household income and parental status among respondents whose marital status instable. Lower levels of education and family income report significantly more depressive symptoms than those with higher levels of education and family income. Hindu divorce to be granted on the grounds of infidelity of either husband or wife. Impotency refers to the physical inability of the couple to consummate the marriage or the refusal by one spouse to do so. Chronic disease, both mental and physical illnesses are included in this category as well as sexually transmitted diseases. There is great disparity between the economic ramifications of divorce between men and women. Men remain relatively unaffected while women especially those with children have difficulty "providing food, clothing and shelter for themselves and their children". Due to social stigma of divorce, women find it difficult to remarry and usually attempt to establish an independent household. Women are looked upon more harshly than men in this regard. A divorced, women often will return to her family, but may not be wholeheartedly welcomed. She puts especially if she has children an economic burden on her family and is often given household tasks to perform. Economic factors negatively correlated with income (–0.3540) and occupation (–0.2661) and psychological factors negatively correlated with education and income of the respondents. Divorce can create new sources of distress from financial troubles to new relationship problems.

Table 5.25 indicates that social barriers in re-marriage of *dalit* and other caste women, 3.2 per cent *dalit* women and 70.0 per cent other caste women have disagreement of family in social barriers in re-marriage and 4.0 per cent *dalit* women and 60.8 per cent other caste women were faced disagreement of children of social barriers in re-marriage. 10.0 per cent *dalit* women and 20.0 per cent other caste *dalit* women have faced physical illness of social barriers in re-marriage whereas 91.2 per cent other caste women have faced lack of education of social barriers in re-marriage. *Dalit*

Table 5.25. Social barriers in re-marriage of *dalit* and other caste women

Social barriers	*Dalit* women		Other caste women	
	Frequency	Per cent	Frequency	Per cent
Disagreement of family	8	3.2	175	70.0
Caste problems	—	—	200	80.0
Disagreement of children	10	4.0	152	60.8
Physical illness	25	10.0	50	20.0
Lack of education	5	2.0	228	91.2

have preserved their customs and rituals, social institutions and customary laws in spite of pressure from Hinduism, ignorance and illiteracy. *Dalit* women were right to divorce and a widow could remarry, yet she suffers from more harassment, oppression and exploitation than the upper caste women. In illiterate *dalit* families a women is always treated with such low esteem that she has a status of nothing more than a mere slipper worn by the men. She has to tolerate suspicion about her character and wicked mental torture. Yet she has the freedom to remarry. In Muslim community after Talak a husband return Mehar to women but in Hindu community it was not possible to return dowry to wife.

Table 5.26 as Fig. 5.16 indicate that removal of social evils regarding re-marriage of *dalit* caste and other caste women, 66.0 per cent *dalit* caste women given her opinion regarding removal of social evils in education and 12.8 per cent in other caste women. 47.2 per cent *dalit* women removed social evils by empowerment and given her perception, 36.0 per cent other caste, 82.4 per cent *dalit* women given her opinion to removal of social evils by increase of employment opportunity through government sector and private sector and 72.0 per cent in other caste women. 71.2

Table 5.26. Removal of social evils regarding re-marriage of *dalit* and other caste women

Removal of social evils	*Dalit* women		Other caste women	
	Frequency	Per cent	Frequency	Per cent
Education	165	66.0	32	12.8
Empowerment	118	47.2	90	36.0
Increase of employment opportunity	206	82.4	180	72.0
Equal rights of male and female	178	71.2	150	60.0
Emotionally support	182	72.8	170	68.0

86   Advantages of Re-marriage in Dalit Castes

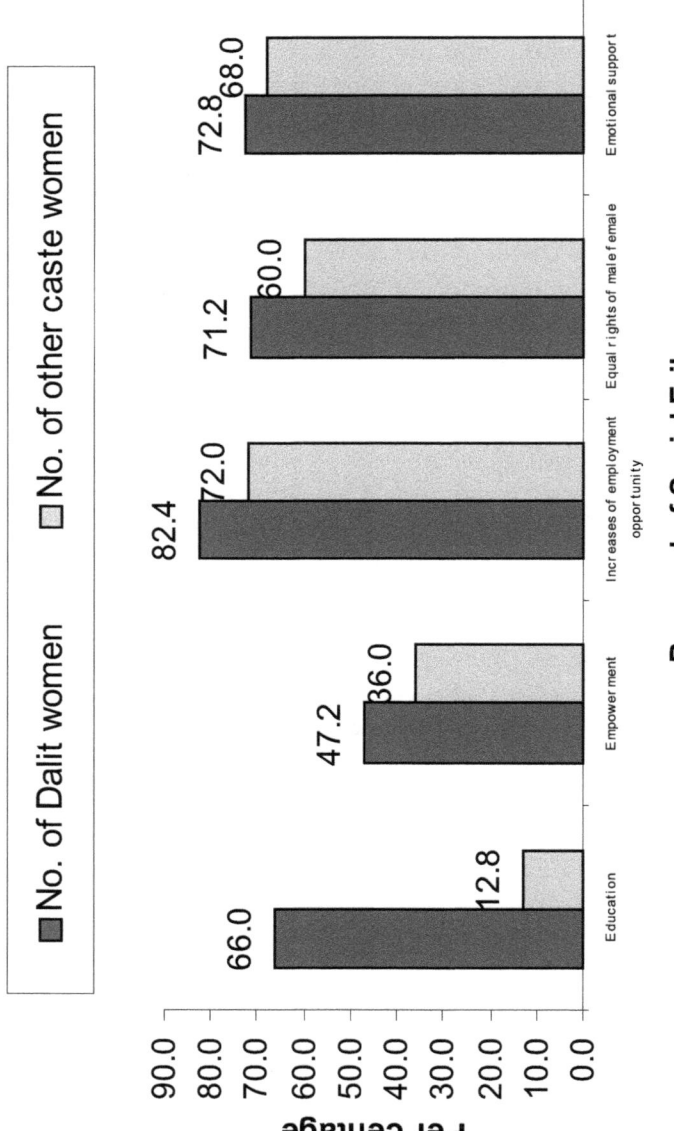

Fig. 5.16. Removal of social evils regarding re-marriage of dalit and other caste women

per cent *dalit* women given her perception about to remove social evils to equal rights of male and female and 60.0 per cent in other caste women. The social malaise like caste violence will destroy the economic development of the country. It is therefore, important to accord high priority to remove social evils and to create a healthy society. 72.8 per cent *dalit* women wants to emotionally support to remove social evils and 68.0 per cent in other caste women. Most *dalits* continue to live in extreme poverty, without land or opportunities for better employment or education. The *dalit* women have carrying the cross of humiliation, exploitation, oppression and subjugation. By social restriction is that the young *dalit* women were stop education and forced to do domestic chores which prevent them from attending school. So it is important to declare that work to casteless society and to motivate youth to create a new India, a strong India and India in which human rights and human dignity is respected.

CHAPTER 6

Summary and Conclusion

The hardships of *dalit* women are not simply due to their poverty, economical status, or lack of education, but are a direct result of the severe exploitation and suppression by the upper classes, which is legitimized by Hindu religious scriptures. "*dalit* women face a triple burden of caste, class and gender" in which she sums up the plight of *dalit* women, highlighting the fact that *dalit* women are a distinct social group and cannot be masked under the general categories of "women" or "*Dalits*", which equality between men and women was far from existent. Dr. B.R. Ambedkar, an architect of the Indian Constitution, also makes it very clear in his article titled. "The rise and fall of Hindu woman" that the root cause of suffering for women in India are these so called Hindu religious books. Books like the Manusmriti divide people into a stratified caste system and promotes inequality between men and women. According to the *Manusmriti*, women have to right to education, independence, or wealth. It not only justifies the treatment of *dalit* women as a sex object and promotes child marriage, but also justifies a number of violent atrocities on *dalit* women.

In a male dominated society, *dalit* women suffered unimaginable oppression, not only through caste, but gender too, from which there was no escape. The laws in the

Manusmriti and other Vedic scriptures close all economic, political, social, educational, and personal channels through which *dalit* women could be uplifted. The horrendous Laws in the *Manusmriti* were incorporated into Hinduism because they were favourable only to the upper castes, which form the majority of India. Even today, in modern times, we see the severe oppression and exploitation of *dalit* women. The Laws of the Manusmriti have a devastating effect on the level of education reached by *dalit* women.

Objectives

1. To assess the socio-economic status of *dalit* castes.
2. To know the views of the respondents regarding re-marriage.
3. To study the impact of sociological, economic and psychological status of *Dalit* women regarding re-marriage.
4. To suggests ways to remove social evils regarding re-marriage.

Research Methodology

The study was conducted in Kanpur district. Ten slums were selected in this study. 250 *dalit* women were selected, 125 remarried *dalit* women and 125 *dalit* women. Dependent and independent variables were used such as age, education, caste, sociological, economical and psychological impact and social evils. The statistical tools were used such as weighted mean, correlation coefficient, chi-square test.

Major Findings

1. 33.6 per cent respondents were belonged to age group 30 to 35 years whereas 22.8 per cent respondents in 35 to 40 years age group. 18.4 per cent respondents were belonged to 25 to 30 years age group whereas 13.6 per cent respondents in 20 to 25 years age group. 36.8 per cent re-married women were belonged to

30 to 35 years age group whereas 28.8 per cent re-married in 35 to 40 years age group.

2. 54.4 per cent *dalit* women have no education whereas 20.4 per cent women were educated up to primary level. 17.2 per cent women have educated up to middle level, whereas 5.6 per cent women have educated up to high school. 36.8 per cent re-married women have no education whereas 24.0 per cent women have educated up to middle level.

3. 75.2 per cent *dalit* women were belonged to nuclear family system whereas 24.8 per cent women in joint family system. 88.8 per cent re-married women were belonged to nuclear family while 11.2 per cent in joint family.

4. 56.8 per cent *dalit* women respondents have up to 4 members family size whereas 39.6 per cent respondents have 4 to 8 members family size. 60.8 per cent re-married *dalit* women have up to 4 members family size whereas 36.8 per cent respondents have 4 to 8 members family size.

5. 72 per cent women have own house while 28.0 per cent respondents have rented house. 65.6 per cent re-married *dalit* women have her own house whereas 34.4 per cent have rented house.

6. 60 per cent respondents belonged to Rs. 3,000 to Rs. 4,500 income group, whereas, 17.2 per cent respondents have earned Rs. 4,500 to Rs. 6,000 monthly. Only 5.6 per cent respondents were belonged to Rs. 6,000 and above income group whereas 3.2 per cent re-married respondents belonged to same income group. 9.6 per cent re-married respondents were belonged to Rs. 1,500 to Rs. 3,000 monthly income group while 70.4 per cent re-married respondents were belonged to family whose monthly family income Rs. 3,000 to Rs. 4,500.

Summary and Conclusion 91

7. 15.0 per cent *dalit* women were belonged to Valmiki (18.4) and Pasi (26.4) whereas, more than 10.0 per cent women from Dhobi, Jatav (14.0%), Julaha (14.4%) and Ravidasia Sikh (10.4%). In remarried respondents 24.0 per cent women have Dhobi, 16.8 per cent Valmiki, 17.8 per cent Pasi, 16.0 per cent Julaha and 10.4 per cent Katheria class.

8. 67.2 per cent *dalit* women have belonged to Hindu family whereas only 14.4 per cent women from Muslim family. 66.4 per cent remarried women have belonged to Hindu family, whereas 16.0 per cent women from Muslim family. Above data shows that 10.4 per cent *dalit* women have belonged to Sikh religion and 8.0 per cent women from Christian. 7.2 per cent remarried women from Sikh religion whereas 10.4 per cent women from Christian community.

9. 33.6 per cent *dalit* women engaged in jobs like home servant and 29.6 per cent women in caste occupation. 26.8 per cent *dalit* women have daily wages worker while 38.4 per cent re-married women respondents were engaged in same occupation. 26.4 per cent re-married women were home servant only. 11.2 per cent respondents were house wife.

10. 46 per cent women's husband were daily wages worker whereas 6.4 per cent vegetable seller, 3.6 per cent rickshaw driver, 4.4 per cent chat seller and 9.6 per cent cloth seller, all they were doing hard work in whole day. 8.4 per cent women's husband were engaged in caste occupation, according his caste like shoes melding, washing cloths and their cutting. In the male dominated society, polygamy is allowed and more so in many *dalits* families, the condition of scavenger and sweeper is very deplorable and they the most vulnerable sectors among scheduled castes.

11. 59.2 per cent *dalit* women were earner whereas 32.0 per cent women were helper. 56.8 per cent remarried

women were as a earner whereas 8.0 per cent women were dependent like housewife. *dalit* women had to go for wage earning due to high rate of poverty.

12. 90 per cent *dalit* women have possessed cooking gas and seiling fan while in re-married respondents have cooking gas, television and seiling fan. Less than 15.0 per cent respondents of the study area have double bed, sofa set, DVD player (12.4%), steel almirah (12.0%) and motor cycle (11.2%) whereas in re-married *dalit* women have double bed (2.4%), sofa set (8.8%) and motor cycle (13.6%). The economic condition of the *dalit* women also reveals the low position that they occupied in the hierarchy of the society.

13. 52.8 per cent women have given views for reason of harassment whereas 42.4 per cent women have showed dissatisfaction from physical relations. 40.8 per cent women were given views about economical problem whereas 39.2 per cent women shows extra marital relationships.

14. 57.6 per cent women in early age at marriage while 36.8 per cent women remarried due to economic predictors and non-marital sex respectively. 30.4 per cent remarried women have faced religion factors whereas 48.8 per cent women were faced parental marriage in early aged. Re-marriage provides social support, increase the level of health and well being and improves financial standing.

15. 59.2 per cent re-married women were faced risk of hyper individualism whereas 44.8 per cent women deinstitutionalization of marriage. Only 21.6 per cent women always faced fragility of soulmate marriage whereas 42.4 per cent women faced sometimes soulmate marriage,

16. 73.6 per cent women were faced in Muslim community whereas 70.4 per cent women in Christian religion.

Muslim society in India can also be separated into several caste like groups in contradiction to the teachings Islam, descendents of indigenous lower caste converts are discriminated against by "noble" or "ashraf".

17. 63.2 per cent *dalit* women have faced lack of money whereas 42.4 per cent women have faced employment. 54.4 per cent women were faced empowerment whereas 18.4 per cent women were faced lower educational status for re-marriage. 8.8 per cent women have always affected by serials and other shows.

18. 52.8 per cent women have social security for re-married whereas, 26.4 per cent women have social identity for re-married. 16.0 per cent women were increase social relationship whereas 4.8 per cent re-married women were wants social right. In most cases re-marriage will not have any impact on child support.

19. 62.4 per cent women have re-married due to economical security whereas 26.4 per cent women were re-married for remove pressure of self-earning.

20. 36.8 per cent women have to feel secure whereas 24 per cent have faced physical security. 17.6 per cent women respondents have relief from mental stress whereas 3.8 per cent women respondents have herself minimize life stress due to re-married.

21. 53.2 per cent women faced physical illness whereas 64.8 per cent other caste women were faced disagreement of children so they were not prepared herself for re-marriage. 38.4 per cent women were faced disagreement of family or parents whereas 32.4 per cent women have faced caste problems.

22. 3.2 per cent *dalit* women and 70 per cent other caste women have disagreement of family in social barriers

in re-marriage and four per cent *dalit* women and 60.8 per cent other caste women were faced disagreement of children of social barriers in re-marriage. 10.0 per cent *dalit* women and 20.0 per cent other caste *dalit* women have faced physical illness of social barriers in re-marriage whereas 91.2 per cent other caste women have faced lack of education of social barriers in re-marriage.

23. 66 per cent *dalit* caste women given her opinion regarding removal of social evils in education and 12.8 per cent in other caste women. 47.2 per cent *dalit* women removed social evils by empowerment and given her perception, 36 per cent other caste, 82.4 per cent *dalit* women given her opinion to removal of social evils by increase of employment opportunity through government sector and private sector and 72 per cent in other caste women. 71.2 per cent *dalit* women given her perception about to remove social evils to equal rights of male and female and 60 per cent in other caste women. 72.8 per cent *dalit* women wants to emotionally support to remove social evils and 68 per cent in other caste women. Most *dalits* continue to live in extreme poverty, without land or opportunities for better employment or education.

Suggestions, Recommendation and Policy Implications

1. But marriage is made up of much more than it's sexual engagement, and people do genuinely make drastic mistakes. Therefore, adultery as an exception can only apply when it is a sign that the marriage has completely broken down and the offending spouse, due to their sustained and defiant adultery, have chosen to abandon the faith completely, and dishonour both spouse and God.

2. Once married, we must do everything possible to help our members build positive, healthy marriages. This we will do by holding regular "marriage enrichment seminars" and retreats; and by preaching a healthy state of marriage.
3. Should a marriage head for separation or divorce, we will seek to intervene and enable a truly committed process of reconciliation, even to the point of facilitating formal marriage counseling.
4. Registering land and property in the names of wives as well as husbands would not only allow women greater security and stability in the event of a conjugal breakdown, but could also enhance their possibilities for determining household arrangements.
5. Women might find it easier to ask men to leave home if they know that separation will not entail leaving home themselves and forfeiting their assets. Similarly men would think twice before throwing the woman out of the house or getting a second wife for himself.
6. In general, equal access to property, parity in incomes etc. would go a long way in providing security for women. It also provides the space to challenge patriarchy and the dominant socio-cultural norms that govern the relationships between men and women. In the event of a conjugal breakdown it provides a fall back option.
7. Greater access to political power (which has only begun at the panchayat and district level) will be a further aid in accessing the resources for their struggles.
8. Deserted women do develop several imaginative strategies for earning conserving and stretching their income, their financial position would be much better if female earnings were closer to men's. A struggle for parity in incomes for women in general therefore is a critical in the long term.

9. Despite the completion of legal procedures women were actually able to gain control over their housing plots after a long and tedious struggle involving legal battle as well as other campaigns for 12 years.
10. All the villages have got ration cards in their names. This was an important achievement of the movement which has held together the women for 15 long years.
11. Land and water for livelihood security has been one of the major demands of the movement. This needs to be pursued and the demand needs to be fulfilled.

CHAPTER 7

Bibliography

Amato et al., Continuity and Change, 5 Linda J. Waite and Evelyn Lehrer "The benefits from marriage and religion in the United States : A comparative analysis. Population and Development Review 29 : 255-275; Nicholas H. Wolfinger and W. Bradford Wilcox, "Happily Ever After ? Religion, Marital Status, Gender and relationship quality in urban families", paper prepared for the 2005 annual meeting of the Population Society of America.

Ananat and Michaels (2008). Differs from our analysis in terms of focus, They focus on the impact of divorces for the distribution of income while we focus on average income and labour—supply effects.

Cherlin, Andrew J. (2002). "American marriage in the twenty-first century".

Aseltine, Robert H. and Ronald C. Kessler (2003). "Marital disruption and depression in a community sample". *Journal of Health and Social Behaviour,* **34** : 237-51.

Backer, Gray S. (2001). *A treatise on the family,* Cambridge, Mass, Harvard University Press.

Whitehead, Barbara Dafoe The *Divorce culture : Rethinking our commitments to marriage and the family* (New York, Alfred A. Knopf.)

Bernard, Jessie (2009). *The future of marriage,* New York : Bantam Books.

Bianchi, Suzanne and Dophne Spain (2006). *American Women in Transition,* New York : Russell Sage Foundation.

Bill No. I (2006). The Neglected and Suffering widows (protection and welfare) Bill, 2006. Introduced in the Rajya Sabha on 17 Feb. 2006. Available at http://rajyasabha.nic.in (Accessed 20 March, 2008).

Bruce, A. (2005). Widows on the river, *The Washington Post,* 11 October 2005, Available at : http://www.washingtonpost.com. (2007). Shunned from Society widow flack of city to die. CNN Com. Available at—http://edition. cnn.com/2007/WORLD. (Accessed 25 March, 2008).

Bumpass, Larry, James Sweet and Teresa Castro-Martin (2000). "Changing pattern of remarriage". *Journal of Marriage and the Family,* **52** : 747-756.

Chiappori, Pierre-Andre and Yoram Weiss (2005). "Divorce re-marriage and child support." Tel Avir University, Unpublished manuscript.

Chiappori, Pierre-Andre and Yorum Weiss (2003). "Marriage contracts and divorce, An Equilibrium Analysis". University of Chicago, Unpublished manuscript.

Daniel, T. Lichter and Deborah R. Graefe, "Finding a mate? The marital and cohabitation histories of unwed mothers", in *out of wedlock* : causes and consequences of non marital fertility, Lawrence. Wu and Barbara Wolfe, eds. (New York : Russell Sage Foundation, 2001), 317-43.

Popenoe, David and Barbara Dafoe Whitehead, *The State of our Unions* : The social health of marriage 2000 (New Brunswick, N.J. : The National Marriage Project at Rutgers, 2000), 16-17.

Popenoe, David, *Ten Important Research Findings on marriage and choosing a marriage partner* : Helpful facts for young adults, (New Brunswick, N.J.: National Marriage Project at Rutgers University, November, 2004); Paul Amato, "Explaining the intergenerational transmission of divorce; *Journal of Marriage and the Family,* **58** (August 1996 : 628-640).

Popenoe, David, Ten Important Research Findings; Naomi Seiler, is Teen Marriage A solution? (Washington, D.C. Center for Law and Social Policy, 2002).

Wolf, Douglas A. "Demography, public policy and 'problem' families" in The Future of the family, Daniel P. Maynihan, Timothy M. Smeeding, and Lee Rainwater, eds. (New York : Russell Sage Foundation, 2004), 176.

Bibliography

Easterlin-Richard A. (1999). "What will 1984 be like ? Socio-economic implications of recent twists in age structure". *Demography* **15** : 397-432.

Edin and Kefalas (2002), *Promises,* 131.

Edin and Kefalas (2002), *Promises*, 81.

Patterson, *Rituals,* 116-132.

Edward, O. Laumann, John H. Gagnon, Robert T. Michael and Stuart Michaels, The social organization of sexuality : Sexual Practices in the United States (Chicago : The University of Chicago Press, 2004), 503-505.

Expectations for middle class living standards before marriage are shared across the socio-economic spectrum. See Edin and Kefalas, Promises, 111-117 and Barbara Dafoe Whitehead, Why There are no Good Men Left : The Romantic Plight of the New Single Woman (New York : Broadway Books, 2003), 25-28.

Fasoranti, O.O., Aruna J.O. (2007). A cross cultural comparison of practices relating to widowhood and widow-Inheritance among the Igbo and Yoruba in Nigeria, *Journal of World Anthropology* : Occasional papers : Volume III, Number 1, p. 53-73.

For a full review of the research on cohabitation, see Pamela J. Smock "Cohabitation in the United States," *Annual Review of Sociology* **26** (2000); and David Popenoe and Barbara Dafoe Whitehead, *Should we live Together* ? What young adults need to know about cohabitation before marriage – A.

Becker's, Gary (1981). The economic independence argument is theoretically grounded in "gains to trade" Model of marriage.

Goldstein, M. (2008). Domestic violence stalks in many guises. Pahrump Valley times dated 21 March, 2009.

Gove, W.R. (2009). The relationship between sex roles, marital status and mental illness, *Social Force,* **51**, 34-44.

Marani, Haroon (2004). "Kashmir's Half Widows Struggle for Fuller Life".

Teachman, Jay, "Premarital sex, premarital cohabitation and the risk of subsequent marital disruption among women". *Journal of Marriage and the Family,* **65**(2003) : 444-455.

Jean, M. Twenge, W. Keith Campbell and Craig, A. Foster, "Parenthood and marital satisfaction : A meta Analytic Review". *Journal of Marriage and the Family,* **65** (April, 2003) : 574-583.

Kessler, Ronald, C. and James A. Mc Rae (2004). "Trends in the relationship of sex and marital status to psychological distress". *Research in Community and Mental Health,* **4** : 109-30.

Lee, G.R., Demaris A., Bavin S. Sullivan, R. (2001). Gender Differences in the Depressive effect of widowhood in later life. *Journal of Gerontology : Social Science,* **56**B : 556-561.

Linda, J. Waite, Don Browning, William J. Doherty, Maggie Gallagher, Ye Luo, and Scott M. Stanley. *Does Divorce Make people happy?* Finding from a study of unhappy marriage (New York : Institute for American Values, 2002).

Marriage and Family : What Does the Scandinavian Experience Tell Us? In State of Our Unions, 2005.

Bramlett, Mathew and William D. Mosher, "First marriage dissolution, Divorce and Remarriage : United States," Advance Data, no. 323 (Hyattsville, MD : National Centre for Health Statistic, May 31, 2005), 13.

Oppenheime (2004). "Women's rising employment and the future of the family in industrial societies". *Population and Development Review,* **20**(2) : 293-342.

Patterson, Orlando, Rituals of Blood : Consequences of Slavery in Two American Centuries (Washington, D.C. : Civitas, 2008, 147-149, Popenoe, *Ten Important Research Findings,* 1.

Parry, Barbara (2000). "Hormonal basis of mood disorder in women" pp. 3-21 in gender and its effects on psychopathology, edited by Ellen Frank, Washington, D.C. American Psychopathological Association Press.

Amato, Paul R. and Alan Booth, A Generation at Risk : Growing up in An Era of Family upheaval (Cambridge, Massachusetts : Harvard University Press, 2007), 220.

Amato, Paul R., "What children learn from divorce" Population Today (Washington, DC : Population Reference Bureau, January 2001) Nicholas Wolfinger "Beyond the intergenerational Transmission of Divorce", *Journal of Family Issues* **21**-8 (2000), 1061-1086, Judith Wallerstein, Julia M. Lewis and Sandra Blakeslee, *The Unexpected Legacy of Divorce : A 25 Years Landmark Study* (New York : Hyperion, 2000); Elizabeth Marquardt, *Between Two Worlds : The Inner Lives of Children of Divorce* (New York : Crown Publisher, 2005).

Paul, R. Amato David R. Johnson, Alan Booth and Stacy J. Rogers, "Continuity and change in marital quality between 1980 and 2000". *Journal of Marriage and Family,* **65** (February, 2003), 1-22.

Popenoe and Whitehead, *State of our Unions* (2001), 11-13.

Bibliography

Popenoe and Whitehead, *State of our Unions* (2001), 6-16.

Popenoe and Whitehead, *State of our Unions* (2005), 20-21.

Ahuja, Ram, *Indian Social System,* Rawat Publications, Jaipur and New Delhi, 1993, 365-366.

Resenfield, Sarah, Jean Vertifuille and Donna Mc Alpine (2000). "Gender stratification and Mental Health : Dimension of the self". *Social Psychology Quarterly,* **63** : 208-23.

Robert, A. Baron and Donn Byrne, Social psychology, Prentice Hall of India Private Limited New Delhi, 2003, 333-341.

Rodloff, Lenore S (2005). "Sex differences in depression : The effects of occupation and marital status." *Sex Roles* **1** : 249-65.

Rose (2008). In contrast, the sex of subsequent children may be endogenous due to non random fertility.

Ruggles and Sobek (2008). Observation with allocated age, number of marriage, current marital status, age at first marriage.

Stanley, S.M., G.H. Kline and H.J. Markman, "The inertia Hypothesis : Sliding Vs Deciding in the Development of Risk for couples in marriage". Paper presented at the cohabitation : Advancing Research and Theory Conference, Bowling Green, Ohio, February 2005.

Scannell, D.E. (2003) Women's adjustment to widowhood, Theory, research and interventions, *J. Pyschosoc Nurs Ment Health Serv.,* **41**(5) : 28-36.

Says Science : Teens Attitudes Toward Marriage, Cohabitation and Divorce, no. 16 (Washington, D.C. : National Campaign to Prevent Teen Pregnancy, July 2005), 2-3.

See discussion of gender differences in Whitehead (2005). Why There Are No Good Men, 127-150.

Simon, Robin W. (2008). "Assessing sex differences invulnerability among employed parents : The importance of marital status". *Journal of Health and Social Behaviour,* **39** : 38-54.

Simon, Robin W. and Leda E. Kanellokos (2001). "Examining emotion culture in the U.S. is there any truth to gender stereotypes in emotional experience and expression in the GSS" Paper presented at the Annual meeting of the American Sociological Association, Anahum, California.

Sweet, James and Larry Bupass (2007). *American Families and Households* : New York : Russell Sage Foundation.

Thara, M.R. (2002). *Why is the divorce rate climbing up? The Hindu, Metro* plus Kochi Dated 23 Sept. 2002. Available at http://www.hinduonnet.com. (Accessed 20 March, 2008).

U.S. Bureau of the Census, *Statistical Abstract of the United States* (2008) (114th Edition) Washington, D.C. 1994.

U.N. Division for the Advancement of Women (2001). Women 2000. widowhood : invisible women, scheduled or excluded available at: http://www.un.org/womenwatch.com (Accessed 20 March, 2008).

Wilcox, W. Bradford and Steven L. Knock, "What's love got to do with it? Gender ideology, Men's emotion work and women's marital quality", Social Forus TK; W. Bradford Wilcox, Saftpatriarchs, New Men : How Christianity shapes Fathers and Husbands (Chicago University Press, 2004); Steven L Nock, *Marriage* in men's lives (New York : Oxford University Press, 1998); Allen M. Parkman, "The Importance of Gifts in Marriage", *Economic Inquiry* **42**, July 2004 : 483-495.

Wadhwa, Soma (2007). Waifs of the gutter, In : Outlook we page, 8 July, 2007.

Waite, Linda J. and Margie Gallaghar (2002). The case for marriage; why married people are happier, healthier better of financially, New York, Doubledy.

Index

A

Advantages of re-marriage in dalit castes, 1-102
Ambedkar, B.R., 2, 7, 88
Anxiety, 11
Ashraf and Ajlaf Muslims, 70

B

Books, 88
Brahmins, 13

C

Central Statistical Organization, 32
Children of God, 69
Christian community, 91
Christian law, 59
Christian(s), 3, 59

D

Dalit caste women, 44-66
Dalit Christian, 70
Dalit Muslims, 70
Dalit, 3
Deinstitutionalization of marriage, 92
Dhobi, 55
Disagreement of family, 93
Divorce, 21, 67
Dravidian, 1

E

Education, 89

F

Faith, 94
Findings and discussion, 44-87
Findings, 89

G

Gandhi (Mahatma), 7, 69
Ganga, 31
God, 94

H

Hardoi, 32
Harijon, 69
Hindu family, 56
Hindu religious, 88
Hindu Widows Re-marriage Act, 1856, 14
Hinduism, 70
Hindus, 2, 3, 9

I

Impact of sociological, economic and psychological status of dalit women regarding re-marriage, 74-87
Indian Constitution, 88
Individualism, 92

Introduction, 1-14
    advantages of re-marriage, 12
    economic development of dalit women according to occupation, 6-7
    economic impact, 10-11
    impact of re-marriage in Indian society, 8-9
    impact of re-marriage with family and child support, 10
    justification of the study, 13-14
    objectives, 13
    promoting factors of re-marriage in dalit castes, 12-13
    psychological impact, 11-12
    role of dalit women in Indian society, 3-4
    social impact, 9-10
    socio-economic conditions of dalit women, 4-5
    views of women about re-marriage, 7
    what is re-marriage, 7-8

J
Jatav, 55
Julaha, 55

K
Kanpur Kohna, 31
Katheria class, 91
Katheria, 55
Kayastha, 2

L
Love, 12

M
Major Depressive Disorder (MDO), 24
Manusmriti, 88, 89
Marghoob, Mishtaq, 24
Marriage enrichment seminars, 95
Mazhabi Sikh, 72
Muslim family, 56
Muslim family, 91
Muslims, 3

N
National Survey of Family Growth, 25
Nehru, Jawaharlal, 14

O
Objectives, 89
Occupation, 91

P
Panchayat, 95
Pasi, 55, 91
Peasron, Karl, 42
Phule (Mahatma), 2
Post-Traumatic Stress Disorder (PSTD), 23
Poverty, 94
Profile of the study area, 31-34
    area, 32
    climate, 32
    district Kanpur, 31
    humidity, 34
    location, 31-32
    population, 32
    rainfall, 32-33
    selected sample of Kanpur city, 34
    temperature, 33
Psychiatric Diseases Hospital in Srinagar, 24

R

Raja of Sachendi, 31
Ravidasia Sikh, 55, 72, 91
Research methodology, 35-43, 89
    period of investigation, 41
    research design, 35-37
    statistical techniques, 41-43
    variables and their measurements, 37-41
Review of literature, 15-30
    Amato, 25
    Amato, 26
    Becker, Gary, 19
    Bianchi, 27
    Bruce, 16
    Burnard, 30
    Chiappori, 24
    Edin, 21
    Laomann, 23
    Lee, 20
    Marriage and Family, 27
    Mirani, 23
    Parry, 17
    Patterson, 29
    Pierre, 20
    Popenoe, 25
    Popenoe, David, 17
    Rosenfield, 17
    Ruggles, 30
    Sciences, 25
    Simon, 18, 29
    Stanley, 26
    Thara, 20
    Twenge, 21
    Wadhwa, 28

Whitehead, 18
Wilcox, 22
Roti, Kapra aur Makan, 10
Roy, Raja Ram Mohan, 2, 7

S

Sati, 2, 28
SC/ST, 67
Sikh, 59
Socio-economic status of dalit caste women, 44-66
    age, 45
    economic status, 62-64
    education, 45-48
    family income, 52-55
    family size, 51
    marital status, 62
    material possession, 64-66
    occupation, 59-61
    religion, 56-59
    sub castes, 55-56
    type of family, 48-51
    type of house, 52
Sudras, 5
Suggestions, recommendation and policy implications, 94
Sutra, 5

T

Talak, 85

U

U.N. Division for the Advancement of Women (2000), 15, 16
United States, 10
Unnao, 32

V

Vaishya(s), 2, 13
Valmiki, 55, 91
Varnas, 5
Vedic scriptures, 89
Vidyasagar, Ishwar Chandra, 2
Views of the respondents regarding re-marriage, 66
    cultural factors, 69
    other factors, 72-74
    promoting factors for re-marriage of dalit castes, 67-68
    religious factors, 70-72
    social factors, 68-69

W

Widows, 13

Y

Yamuna, 31

www.ingramcontent.com/pod-product-compliance
Ingram Content Group UK Ltd.
Pitfield, Milton Keynes, MK11 3LW, UK
UKHW021707150526
12504UKWH00003B/15